INSIGHT

A Christian's Guide to Spiritual Maturity

Written by Carla Jean Hull
Through Inspiration of The Holy Spirit

INSIGHT
A Christian's Guide to Spiritual Maturity
Written by Carla Jean Hull
Through Inspiration of The Holy Spirit

TRU Statement Publications supports the right to free expression and the value of copyright. The purpose of copyright is to encourage writers and artist to produce the creative works that will leave a timeless impression of humanity.

The scanning, uploading, and distribution of this book without written permission is a theft of the author's intellectual property. If you would like permission to use materials from the book (other than for a review), please contact
cjhforchrist@gmail.com.com.

Thank you for your support of the author's rights.

Cover photograph by © Kokhanchikov, Adobe Stock

Unless otherwise stated, all scripture quotations of the Holy Bible have been taken from the King James Version (KJV)

Book Completion Services Provided by:
TRU Statement Publications | www.trustatementpublications.com

Copyright © 2021 Carla Jean Hull
Frist Edition: April 2021
Printed in the United States of America
0 4 1 5 2 0 2 1
ISBN: 978-1-948085-52-6

DEDICATION

I want to thank The Holy Spirit for His anointing that I believe will be on this book, which He inspired. I love You, Lord.

I also want to thank my husband, Pastor Richard S. Hull Jr. for all his support and help in researching scriptures. Thank you, honey, for asking me many times, "Have you worked on your book yet today?" I love you handsome.

I want to thank my granddaughter, Julia Rosemarie Ortega, for all her technical support. I love you, Julz.

Last but not least, my thanks to my best friend of 30 years, Rev. Linda Robinson, for writing the foreword for this book. It's been a long time coming. I love you, BFFE.

CONTENTS

FOREWORD ....
   By Rev. Linda Robinson.. i

INTRODUCTION ....
   Why This Book? iii

CHAPTER ONE ....
   Walking by Faith 1

CHAPTER TWO ....
   The Armour of God 25

CHAPTER THREE ....
   Spiritual Warfare-Defeating The Enemy 31

CHAPTER FOUR ....
   Prayer | Intercession | Fasting 45

CHAPTER FIVE ....
   Sacrifice & Obedience 51

CHAPTER SIX ....
   Spiritual Gifts 59

CHAPTER SEVEN ....
   The Fruit of The Spirit 67

CHAPTER EIGHT ....
   Hearing From God 73

CHAPTER NINE ....
   Troubles, Trials, and Temptations 81

CHAPTER TEN ....
    Trusting God 89

CHAPTER ELEVEN...
    The Harvest/Winning Souls 93

CHAPTER TWELVE...
    Sin/Separation From God & Unforgiveness 99

CHAPTER THIRTEEN ....
    Live Ready... 103

CHAPTER FOURTEEN ....
    It's Time to Grow 109

CHAPTER FIFTEEN..
    The Salvation Chapter 113

APPENDIX 117

GOSPEL HANDOUT 119

FOREWORD
By Rev. Linda Robinson

It gives me great pleasure to write in this book. Carla Jean has been a dear friend of mine for almost thirty years! Wow, where does the time go?

I think I'd like to start by saying I'm so proud of Carla and impressed for so many reasons and on multiple levels. I've watched her as she has gone through many life struggles. It has been an amazing journey and through it all God has been her constant companion. She seeks out the divine will of God, whether it be in finance, child raising, divorce, or re-marriage. God is her pilot in every facet of her life.

That's why this book is so God designed. For those who will read this book, you will find excellent direction and answers for life's situations. I thoroughly enjoyed every chapter! I'm so excited to see what this wonderful author, Carla Jean Hull, will do next for God?

I love you, my BFFE—Best Friends For-Ever!

INTRODUCTION
Why This Book?

I started writing this book some years ago, and I don't really remember why I began writing it. I'm pretty sure I wanted to share some insight (revelation knowledge) that I was receiving from The Lord about waiting and walking by faith. I had even wondered if God had given me the gift of faith. I had asked Him that. So, I began writing. And then I got stuck. I didn't know why.

It was during a time in my life that I totally had to depend on God and His Word to get me through. He initially said to me, "*Be still,*" and I said, "Yes Lord."

I waited on God. For ten years. I prayed, fasted, trusted, and believed. I waited. And then my miraculous breakthrough came. It seemed soon and suddenly when it finally happened!

During those 10 years of waiting, it felt like I had all the faith for that situation. No one could deter my faith. My faith helped me to have peace and to stand strong. I think that was God's plan all along. To help me wait so I could receive my miracle in His perfect timing. If I had not waited, I could have put myself in another bad situation.

Waiting on The Lord was an honor—Is an honor. The Holy God, Creator of heaven and earth had asked "me" to wait on Him. I trusted Him, but I needed His help to wait without wavering. He gave me that help. As the Word of God says it will do. My waiting on The Lord renewed my strength. He spoke and revealed things to me that helped me stand strong. Praise God for His insight!

On Insight/Revelation Knowledge:

God gave me the title, subtitle, and chapter names for this book. I woke up in the middle of the night and He said, *"You have been stuck because what you have written so far is not your book, but the first chapter of your book."*

I had thought that I was writing a book on faith, which really fit at the time because I was doing some major "walking by faith" believing for my miracle. I knew that God put writing a book on my heart, and I knew I was to write about faith, but as I went along, I realized my book on faith would not be a large book like I had first imagined.

I then started thinking of different ways I might put my writings together. Maybe I would write on different topics in the bible, i.e., the fruit of the spirit, the armour of God, etc. I could then put together a "set" of smaller books. I wasn't sure, but I did like the idea.

It was probably close to a year after having these ideas that God woke me up in the early morning hours, somewhere

INTRODUCTION

between 1:00 and 3:00 a.m. God seems to like 3:00 a.m. It's probably the quietest time of the night. As soon as I woke up, I clearly heard Him speak to me about my book.

I quickly grabbed my phone to send myself a text, because I knew I would not be able to remember all the chapter titles He was giving me. I'm so glad I did. He then gave me the title:

INSIGHT, and the subtitle,

A CHRISTIANS GUIDE TO SPIRITUAL MATURITY.

I wondered if the title was correct, but God soon confirmed it to me. It seemed as if everywhere I looked I saw the word *insight*. It was even in my first chapter that I had written 8 years before. I had no idea until I re-read it.

It began to make sense to me. Over the years, God had given me many moments of "revelation knowledge." He taught me so much! Things I had never realized. The revelation knowledge God had given me, of course gave me supernatural insight. I began to share these "light bulb" moments with others, many times testifying of them during church services at the church I was attending.

Sometimes people would approach me after service to thank me. Of course, sharing revelation knowledge that God had given to me blessed others as well. It was His wisdom, His knowledge, and His insight. It came straight from The Holy Spirit. What a blessing! What a help!

Now, I want to share some of those words of wisdom with

INSIGHT

you too. I hope you are blessed and that you will grow by reading this anointed (I pray) book that God has ordained for such a time as this!

In Christ,

Carla Jean Hull, Author

CHAPTER ONE
Walking by Faith

I love the song that Carman Lucianno sang, *Step of Faith*. It says, "Stepping out on nothing and finding something there" (and) "telling the doubt to wait." That, my friend, is faith. It's not a cop out or just a crutch, as some would say, but it is believing what you can't see.

Do you really have to be able to see something to know that it is there? Sometimes it is right around the corner, just out of sight. I know I've experienced it because I chose to believe and wait on God.

Peter is a great example to us. The way he ignored the storm that was all around them and kept his eyes on Jesus. He believed without doubting and walked on water with Jesus! The others were in the same boat, literally going through the exact same storm. But instead of believing as Peter did, they cried out in fear.

The Word of God says *without faith, we cannot please God* (Hebrews 11:6). It also tells us we do not go through just anything but *what is common to all our brothers and sisters around the world* (1 Corinthians 10:13). What makes the difference is our attitude.

Are we walking by faith or by sight? Scripture instructs us to walk by faith. Peter walked by faith, the others by sight. Although not perfect by any means, I'm sure this event changed Peter for the better. What an example he was to the others that day! It would have been unbelievable if they hadn't seen it for themselves. Watching Peter walk on water with Jesus must have increased their faith too. It had to.

The stresses of this life are many. What good can come from any of them? We can believe that God will bring good out of what the enemy means for harm, just as Joseph said to his brothers in Genesis 50:20 KJV, *"But as for you, ye thought evil against me; but God meant it unto good, to bring to pass, as it is this day, to save much people alive."*

We've all heard things like, "What doesn't kill you will only make you stronger" or "We learn from our mistakes." But is this really true? Well, in my life experiences, I would have to agree and say yes. We realize that good can come from many things that would be perceived as hard or undesirable.

Surgery can correct things in our physical bodies, but it isn't without a process which includes much pain and discomfort. During recuperation we begin to heal, and over time we reap the benefits of enduring it all. We trust what the doctors tell us and believe we will improve. We don't doubt it. That is faith.

Spiritual "surgery" also corrects many things, but in our spiritual and emotional lives God calls these surgeries trials, tests, fires, storms, etc. We sometimes feel that we are in a very low valley, but please remember this is where the most growth takes place.

As we endure going through our tests and not praying ourselves out but through them, we learn what God wants to teach us during those times and we reap the blessings of God. All of these things are easier when done through faith. So much easier!

I can remember, even as a child, having to deal with things that caused great stress in my very young life. Coping then, without the maturity and knowledge I have today, was much more difficult for me. But, because of my Lord and Savior, Jesus Christ, I have grown spiritually to a point where I can realize and recognize the enemy's tricks (you will learn more on this subject in chapter 2).

I have learned that I have absolute authority, in Jesus' name, even to send demons to flight and to overcome whatever the obstacle. I believe. I trust. I have faith. You can too! It really is possible to *walk by faith and not by sight*, just as the Word of God states and instructs (2 Corinthians 5:7).

It is also possible to avoid living by our emotions. This is great insight. It comes from The Holy Spirit. How many of us have ever allowed our emotions to lead us? I know I can raise my hand. Remember, it is a trick of the enemy to get us sidetracked emotionally with things we can't control. So don't try. We need to learn how to give things into God's capable and mighty hands.

INSIGHT

Do we get "caught up in the moment?" Of course we do. But it is possible to overcome that, too. One day at a time. This is a challenge in my own life. I want to have control of myself at all times! Self-control, a fruit of The Spirit (see chapter 3). Evidence that The Holy Spirit dwells in us. One day at a time, I will get there too. I believe it.

God sees my heart. He is my Helper. He will enable me to be victorious in this area too. Because He sees my efforts and He knows my heart, He will make sure that I succeed. I'm closer to that goal today than I was yesterday! Praise God!

Asking God for His help and recognizing when we are being put to the test helps, but it is still very challenging. This also takes faith. It takes an abundant amount of trust in God. It is not easy, especially when our emotions get involved, but it is possible. You need a made-up mind.

I'm going to believe, no matter what! No matter what others say, no matter the circumstances, no matter how it feels. Then, through faith, trust, praise, and being faithful to wait, watch God work on your behalf.

God will lead us and allow us to be tested in this and other areas, but He will be teaching us and refining us through it all. In the end, it is all well worth it. I call this *Spiritual Boot Camp*. It takes strength, stamina, determination, commitment, and self-discipline.

If you want to be called a warrior of God, you cannot be a quitter. You may stumble or even fall from time to time, but get right back up. Be brave, be courageous, as a good soldier *fighting the good fight of faith* (1 Timothy 6:12).

The other soldiers in God's army, all around the world, are in the same fight as you are. We are to be there for each other. We don't abandon each other. We pick each other up gently without causing more damage to each other.

We don't judge because we know that we have been there and could potentially be there again. Trusting God is the answer and will get us through this war. God is our Commander and as long as we obey and follow His leadership, we will be victorious.

The Word of God confirms that any form of anxiety, fear, or worry is not of God, but from our enemy. Worry has never done anyone any good. It doesn't help at all. In fact, it just causes more anxiety. But to almost never *worry*? Sounds great! But possible? Yes, I believe it is! *We can do all things through Christ who strengthens us* (Philippians 4:13).

He is always with us just waiting to help, but He wants us to do what we can, too. It takes time to grow, but if you keep pressing forward, you will absolutely grow. Seems to be easier said than done, doesn't it? The answer would be yes if we try to do it in our own strength.

But, when you learn to lean on God and His strength, it becomes a totally different situation. I pray that many believers can learn this, to trust Him completely, in all kinds of circumstances. You will be tested but hold on and just believe with expectation.

God's Word is true and *will not return to Him void* (Isaiah 55:11). God's Word says to *be anxious for nothing, but pray about everything* (Philippians 4:6). That means not to worry about anything and put your trust fully in God. Worry and fear are the opposite of faith.

Take up that shield of faith that is a part of our armour. We are in the army of God. We are warriors! Fight the good fight of faith! We are on the winning side! And the devil knows it! Praise God!

The word also tells us that *without faith it is impossible to please God* (Hebrews 11:6). I don't know about you, but I really strive to please God on a daily basis. I want to be full of faith in the sight of God. It is a top priority, right along with winning souls, which has become the absolute #1 priority in my ministry for The Lord and in my life.

It is obvious that we have a short time before Jesus raptures the church and we need to put our focus on the harvest. That is, those who are ready to be plucked out of the devil's grip. Those who are ready to say yes to Jesus, salvation, and eternal life but needs someone to guide them. The people that make up the harvest want to go to heaven. Just ask them (see chapter 3 for more on the harvest & winning souls).

When I stand before God, I want to see a big smile on His face and hear those cherished and priceless words, "*Enter in, thou good and faithful servant* (Matthew 25:21)." I am so looking forward to looking Jesus in the face, hugging Him, touching His hair, and falling at His feet! That thought makes me smile! To be in His Presence forever will be more awesome than we can possibly imagine, I know it's going to be great!

I always say that the first thing I want to do is hug Jesus because it will only be because of Him that I even get to enter heaven's gates. I want to thank Him big time! Bow at His feet. The second thing is to see God on his throne and to see The Holy Spirit. The next thing is to meet my son!

I'll take this time to share a sweet testimony. I have told people for quite some time now, of my desire to hug Jesus when I get to heaven. Even if I stand there hugging Him for a thousand years. *A thousand years is as a day with the Lord* (2 Peter 3:8). Even bowed at His feet for the 1st thousand years.

What peace, what comfort, what joy! Why? Because I love Him so much! I am so thankful that He took my punishment and gave me eternal life! After that, I want to see God's Throne and Him sitting on it with all the angels worshipping around Him.

I always tell others I want to see my son, who had passed away as an infant. He had a heart defect and only lived 12 days. I have always dreamed of seeing him again. I know he has been safe with God all these years. One day God gave me a beautiful vision. I was standing in heaven, hugging Jesus. All of a sudden Jesus asked me, *"Carla, would you like to meet your son now?"*

I hadn't even thought of him yet. With excitement, I said,

INSIGHT

"Yes! Jesus! Can You get him for me?"

Then Jesus replied very sweetly, *"Turn around."* I knew my son was standing right behind me! The vision ended there before turning around. It's like waiting to open a special gift. I love surprises! I'm looking forward to that day. I know it will take place just like that! Praise God!

One thing God has so graciously taught me is the difference between faith and trust. This lesson, as with all others, did not come to me on a silver platter, but through pain. The difference between faith and trust? Faith is believing He will do it *without doubting* (Matthew 21:22), whatever it looks like, however long it takes, no matter the opinions of the naysayers because *we walk by faith, not by sight*. This is more than believing that He can do it, but belief that He will do it.

Trust, however, is knowing whatever the outcome, it is the right answer for me in this situation. Continuing to trust God with it, even if I don't like it, is the key. Even if I'm unsure of the outcome, or the path to get there, I trust The Lord. Even when it is uncomfortable, I choose to trust The Lord.

One day, I realized that it was a choice to trust God. The only other alternative is to not trust Him. That was not and is not an option for me. It's more than trusting that everything will be ok, it's trusting Him even when things are not ok.

As I began to write this book, there were many trials going on in my life. I absolutely believe that they were being allowed for a perfect purpose. God directs my steps and no one else. I whole heartedly believe that. I do my best to obey Him and stay out of His way. This is very important.

We cannot fix anything the way God can. He has perfect timing. My job is to wait, trust, obey, and praise Him as I go through this process. I do what is required of me, to the best of my ability, and then leave the outcome to God. If He wants me to remain in these trials, I will be here. I believe it is because He wants to bless me with better. To do good for me and not to harm me.

God wants to strengthen us so we are better able to stand. To stand in these last days. To stand in the face of adversity and to fight the good fight of faith! I believe God wants to use me as one of His examples! What a privilege! It takes a willing heart to let God use you as He chooses.

Because I trust God, I don't pray myself out of my trials but through them. I pray His will be done and that I will be victorious and will learn what He is teaching me through it all. That's different from praying ourselves out of an obvious demonic attack.

I know the Holy Scriptures, which are able to *make me wise unto salvation* (2 Timothy 3:15) and they tell me that *I am blessed when I endure temptation* (James 1:12). I am blessed going in and I am blessed going out. The bottom line for me again is either I trust God, or I don't. I choose to trust Him. He's my Heavenly Father. Didn't I trust my earthly father? My dad? I did! Then how could I ever declare that I don't trust God? He knows I do.

INSIGHT

God knows my heart, and He knows yours too. Why would I not trust the Creator of heaven and earth? Why not trust the one and only true and living God? Who better to put my trust in? Man? Of course not. If any person will bless me, it will be through God's unctioning.

The Word of God says that others will give to me, and they do. God says *He will even take from the wicked and give to the righteous* (Proverbs 13:22). I believe it! God's word is true, and we can stand on His promises at all times. Just believe.

One of the first lessons God taught me through a very challenging time was to <u>be still</u> and know that He is God (Psalm 46:10). God taught me so many things through that season in my life. He taught me to depend on Him, my Provider, and not on man any longer. I have learned to do that. I depend only on God.

What freedom that can bring when you are not waiting on man to meet your needs, but on an all-knowing God. He always comes through. Maybe not when I want, but with perfect timing. I'm learning to wait in faith and expectation. *They that wait upon the Lord shall renew their strength* (Isaiah 40:31 KJV).

Again, God has taught me to depend and wait on Him with expectancy. When we expect God to move on our behalf and begin praising Him for it ahead of time, He will not ignore that. The key here once again is to believe without wavering. He will not allow His children to be ashamed, especially when we have been proclaiming His promises to others. That is for sure!

I get so excited at this knowledge as I have experienced it over and over again. I know it's true. I will continue to profess my faith in my God for the promises He has given me. I stand on His Word, which *will not return to Him void* (Isaiah 55:11). I love that whole scripture. What encouragement it gives to me.

Here is one of my favorite testimonies of waiting on The Lord during a trying time (the short version). When my first husband left me, the first thing I remember that The Lord told me was to "*be still.*" I knew exactly what He was saying to me. He also said, "*Do not look to the left or the right.*"

I answered Him and said, "Ok Lord, I will not even have a cup of coffee with another man." And so, for 10 years I kept my eyes on The Lord, waiting for His will in my life to be done.

Did the Lord come through for me? Yes, He sure did, big time! One day, my miracle breakthrough happened. All of a sudden! God set me free from waiting and gave me one of my most precious gifts. My current husband, Pastor Richard S. Hull Jr. And just let me tell you, he was definitely worth the wait!

The Bible says that it is impossible for God to lie. *He is not a man that He should lie* (Numbers 23:19). The Bible is God's Word, right? And you believe it is true? All of it? If the answer is yes, then why not live your life like it, believing and relying on what The Word of God, THE BIBLE says? I am learning to do just that.

Since it says in The Bible that "*Greater is He that is in me than he that is in the world,"* then it is the absolute truth! It also says that *"Through Christ I can do all things,"* then that is also the absolute truth! What other scriptures come to your mind that you would like to stand on? Go ahead! Try God at His Word. It will not return to Him void!

I decided that if worry is the opposite of faith, and that without faith you cannot please God, then worry had to stop being a part of my life. My goals are to make it to heaven, to take as many with me as I possibly can, and to please God as much as possible while I am still here.

To me, that means I have to walk in faith on a daily basis. So, words and phrases like "but" and "what if" had to leave my vocabulary for good. I resist the negative, refuse the negative, and turn a deaf ear to the negative. Negative talk is not only offensive to me, but it is offensive to God. It is the opposite of faith talk.

But remember, don't just talk faith, walk by faith, f*or faith without works is dead* (James 2:17). Lacking power to move or respond (Websters Dictionary). Be an optimist. We are to *speak life with our tongues and not death* (Proverbs 18:21). This is very helpful in walking by faith. Faith brings with it the peace of God.

Because we are believing for good things to come, we can hold our head up, smile and move forward in expectation. The Word says that *there is a peace that surpasses all understanding* (Philippians 4:7). What a gift! And it is available to us all, just for the asking. Ask and believe to receive.

Not everyone understands this type of faith and the peace of God that is evident from it. They sometimes see it as denial, or that you may not be good at facing reality. They may even see it as you just don't care or wonder what's wrong with that person? Don't they see what's going on?

Well, that must be what it sometimes looks like when *we walk by faith, and not by sight* (2 Corinthians 5:7). That must be what it sometimes looks like when *we lean not on our own understanding* (Proverbs 3:5). That must be what it sometimes looks like when we choose to trust God and His promises. That must be what it looks like when we *raise our shield of faith and it quenches all the fiery darts of the enemy* (Ephesians 6:16). That must be the peace that the bible speaks of. Praise God!

We must remember, faith does not keep us from going through the storms but equips us to go through victoriously and more easily. It absolutely does! Pray yourself through the storms, not out of the storms. We know storms are temporary, with some lasting longer than others and stronger than others, they can seem to be overtaking us, but remember that God will be in control as He sees your faith and trust in Him.

Stay focused. Keep your focus on God, trust Him, and His faithfulness. He will take you forward. He will get you through to the other side.

Then you will see clearly and rejoice that The Lord God was up to something good all along. Don't murmur and complain, which gets you nowhere fast. It postpones our promises from coming through. The Word tells us that praise is what will take us through our hard times much quicker. Give God praise "through" it all. Because He is more than worthy.

Remember Moses and the Israelites in the wilderness? It was supposed to take them only days to get to the promised land. But instead, they walked in circles for 40 years! That was because of their murmuring and complaining. Murmuring and complaining against God even. God, who had rescued them from slavery, through miracles, signs, and wonders. God only had good plans for them.

Because of their defiance and disobedience, their promise was put on hold by God. That journey would have only taken a few days if they had continued to praise and trust God. They needed to keep their focus on The Lord, especially through the wilderness. The same is true for us today. This is a good reminder to praise God through our trials and tribulations!

God did so many miracles for those people, and still they rebelled and sinned against God. It wasn't enough for them. Don't be like them. Appreciate all that God has done for you. Take inventory. Yes, count your blessings and show Him your appreciation. You can do that through praise and worship. Through obedience, you will find your reward.

God is looking for people who will love and serve Him through it all. Through thick and thin. Are you a "fair weathered" friend of God? In other words, as long as things don't get too rough, you serve Him. But when the storms of life get rough, you have second thoughts about living for God.

That kind of commitment will get you nowhere with God and only jeopardizes your eternity. That is not what God is looking for in His people. He is looking for those who will trust Him and obey no matter what road this life takes you down. Those are the ones that will make it in the end. What a blessing it is to know that you are one of His faithful followers. One of the chosen few. *For many are called but few are chosen* (Matthew 22:14 KJV).

To help yourself and others, read and study the Bible daily, pray, go to church to assemble with believers, listen to praise and worship music and talk to other believers that are able to pray with you and be an encouragement to you. Be careful, as some Christians are not strong enough yet to carry their own burdens and be an encouragement to others too.

Make sure you are spending time with a stronger, more mature Christian. Find a mentor, a spiritual parent. We all benefit from this. Everyone needs a confidant that they can trust and will not steer them wrong. Someone who will help to lead your thinking back to God.

Without staying focused on God, we will sink as Peter did. We need to get focused and then stay focused on Jesus. It is so much easier going through our storms this way. We can actually go through smiling because we know that we know that we know God is in control!

There is great faith and there is small faith, but the word of

INSIGHT

God says that even *faith as a grain of a mustard seed* can receive answers from God. Nothing is impossible to those who believe. It only takes small faith to believe enough. Make up your mind that you are going to believe. It's a choice. It really is.

I had a friend I was witnessing to hoping to lead her to salvation through Christ Jesus. She said to me, "Carla, I'm just not sure what exactly I believe."

I answered her and said, "Well, the bible says it just takes a little bit of faith."

She immediately replied, "Oh! I can do that!" and she gave her heart to Jesus. She was born again that day. Praise God!

A lot of our walk with God has to do with free choices. We choose to serve God or not to serve God. We choose to forgive so *that we too can be forgiven* (Mark 11:26 KJV). We choose to smile as we walk through our fires, storms, and tests. We choose to praise Him through it all. We choose to trust God.

We even choose our destiny by either choosing Christ and entering into eternal rest with God or to reject God's Son and spend eternity in the lake of fire where God's presence is absent forever. It's a choice! Your choice! If God is calling you, be alert! Be ready to answer that call while you can. The day is coming when that option will be over.

Let me tell you, there is nothing wrong and there is plenty right in choosing to trust in The Lord! You can know the storm is all around you and still keep your focus on The Lord Jesus

Christ. I love that! What peace He brings.

Isn't that what the Word teaches us? To walk by faith and not by sight? Then why all the doubters? Even among Christians. God still does miracles, and if you want to call this a "miracle of faith," good call! There is a gift of faith and it is tremendous! Even though the gift of faith comes with plenty of trials, I can honestly say, it is well worth it.

When the disciples were in the boat together and saw Jesus walking towards them on the water, they were frightened. But Peter actually stepped out of the boat onto the water and began walking to Jesus.

It wasn't until Peter lost his focus that he began to sink. He lost his focus because of the storm that was all around him. It had distracted him and allowed fear to enter in. We need to stay focused on Jesus as we go through the storms of life.

When we do, we too can learn to walk (by faith) as on water with Jesus, taking one step of faith at a time. How would that apply in your life today? Have you lost your job? Your home? Going through divorce? Lost a loved one? Have a terminal illness? Do you have children you are concerned about? Are you uncertain about your future? Are you being tested and tried?

These are all storms in life, and God's word says not to *think it strange, the fiery trial which has come to try you* (1 Peter 4:12). The Word also says that no temptation has taken you but what is common to mankind. That with every temptation, God will provide a way of escape. We have to acknowledge and take that escape route.

All your brothers and sisters throughout the world are going through the same sort of tests (1 Corinthians 10:13). So, pray one for another. Whatever you are going through, someone else is too. Pray for them the same as you pray for yourself.

If you can stay focused on Jesus and don't give up, you too can walk by faith and not sink, fall, or fail. If you can trust Him, you can have that *peace that surpasses all understanding* (Philippians 4:7). But if you do fall, ask forgiveness, get up and try again. Because of Jesus, we are living under grace, but we are not to trample on God's grace by taking it for granted.

As the other disciples were in awe at what they were watching while Peter stepped out of the boat and actually was walking on the water with Jesus, others also will be in awe at what they see when you too can go through the storm, walking above it, through it, while all along staying focused on Jesus. What a great example of faith in God that is.

Faith or fear? Which do you have more of? When we get upsetting information, initially the fear tries to grab us, but we don't have to allow it to hold on for long. It is challenging to change your thinking, but you can. If you lose your job, can you have faith that God will provide another one and even a better one for you?

If you are given a bad report from the doctor, do you take it as the final answer or do you immediately begin believing God will change that diagnosis, one way or another? Do you allow God to use your situation as a testimony to glorify Himself? I have learned that as you choose to do the right job, God will enable you to be successful in it. Choose—Faith or fear? Which one do you want to walk in? I choose faith.

I know that the spirit of doubt will try to step in to discourage, but we don't have to receive it. We can allow our trials to be steppingstones that take us closer to God rather than stumbling blocks that take us further away from Him. That is a choice too.

That is why we use the *Armour of God* (Ephesians 6). I use my shield of faith daily. Sometimes even literally holding out my invisible, but real, shield of faith and speaking out loud, "Shield of Faith, activate!" I try to remember to do this as soon as I sense a negative thought trying to come toward me. It works! Because I believe it will, and God honors my step of faith. We are to wear the whole Armour of God 24/7, putting it on with prayer.

It is so exciting when The Holy Spirit gives His revelation knowledge to us. Each revelation makes it easier to walk by faith. He knows how to strengthen His children. He knows us all individually. He knows what is best for each of us, at all times. He knows that we are in a spiritual battle and that we need spiritual knowledge to fight it.

We also need to remember that we are in a spiritual battle. We need to learn to fight it spiritually. That *comes by faith, and faith comes by hearing God's Word* (Romans 10:17). That is where our knowledge will come from. That is the best way to be victorious. Even Jesus defeated the devil using scripture.

The bible is our sword. A part of our armour. Hebrews 4:12 says, *"For the word of God is quick, powerful, and sharper than any two- edged sword, piercing even to the dividing asunder of soul and spirit, and of the joints and marrow, and is a discerner of the thoughts and intents of the heart."* Use it daily (also see Ephesians 6).

We have authority to speak and prophesy to the wind. We are told in God's Word that we can speak life to our situations. Walking by faith once again with the authority of our words and not backing down. Speaking what isn't as if it is!

Continue to profess what God has promised: *I am more than a conqueror; I can do all things through Christ who strengthens me; I am the head and not the tail and all that I do will prosper, in Jesus' name! My family will be saved! I am blessed and highly favored of God. I believe it! My barrel shall not run dry…* and on and on.

I am so excited to be writing this book. Here in this chapter, I focus on faith, the biggest lesson I have been learning in the past years. To walk by faith in a much deeper understanding. I have definitely been growing and learning to walk by faith, and so can you! I have learned to practice faith.

When the opportunity arises, I think to myself and tell God, here is my chance to practice what I preach. Here is an opportunity to walk the walk, not just talk the talk! The Word says to encourage yourself daily. I do that, but even then, a battle is a battle, and it has to be fought. It's not easy, but it is doable. Especially when you stand on God's word.

Whose report will you believe? It is a choice. Talk to God about it. He is your helper. He is your strength. Remember, *the battle belongs to the Lord* (2 Chronicles 20:15) He walks with you. He holds your hand, and if needed, He will carry you. You can trust God to be there at all times.

Our Savior Jesus Christ, through His blood, has given us complete access to our Heavenly Father. It is in Jesus' name we pray and are heard. Isn't that remarkable? The Creator of heaven and earth has time for us? Loves us? Wants us? Thinks about us and hurts for us? Rejoices with us and yearns to hear from us? Do you also yearn to hear from Him?

It is *by faith through grace that we are saved* (Ephesians 2:8) and blessed with this personal relationship with God—The Father, God—The Son, and God—The Holy Spirit, all three in one. You can have open communication with Him as long as you go through His one and only begotten Son, Jesus Christ.

If you think about it, everything takes faith. Faith just means to believe without doubting. It took faith to get out of bed this morning and to take your first steps of the day. We knew without doubting that our legs would work. We have faith that our car is going to start. We believe we will see the sunrise, etc.

So, do we have to fight to believe God? Yes! We are fighting a real enemy and it takes faith to defeat him. (See chapters 2 & 3 for more ways to defeat the enemy of our souls.) *Not by might, nor by power, but by My Spirit saith the Lord of hosts* (Zechariah 4:6 (a) KJV).

I do not believe in giving the enemy any more recognition than is necessary. Yes, The Word warns us of his tricks and deceit, and I am very alert to them. Also, we are told that he is the father of lies and the author of confusion, and so forth. I know this is true, but I will not give him too much credit outwardly, I think he enjoys it too much.

It is like the terrorists always trying to take the credit when bad things happen, and they had nothing to do with it. They love the recognition. They love placing fear in others. I believe the devil is the same. So, I fight him more than I speak of him, except to teach others how to defeat him. One of my favorite things to do! And he hates it. Praise God!

So, I ask again, as I did in the beginning of this chapter. Do you have to see something to believe it is there? Can you see the air? Love? No, but we feel them both and we see their effects. It's the same with God. We can't see Him, but it is possible to feel His presence and we see the effects He has on people's lives. I love Him who I have never seen, with all my heart.

End of Chapter Thoughts: In what ways has God helped you to walk by faith and not by the circumstances you see all around you? How has this changed your relationship with God for the better? How has it improved your life?

INSIGHT

CHAPTER TWO
The Armour of God

Put on the whole Armour of God, our spiritual armour, because we do not fight against flesh and blood but against spiritual wickedness. Ephesians chapter 6 verses 10-18 in the King James Version says it this way:

[10] Finally, my brethren, be strong in the Lord, and in the power of His might. [11] Put on the whole armour of God, that ye may be able to stand against the wiles of the devil. [12] For we wrestle not against flesh and blood, but against principalities, against powers, against the rulers of the darkness of this world, against spiritual wickedness in high places. [13] Wherefore take unto you the whole armour of God, that ye may be able to withstand in the evil day, and having done all, to stand. [14] Stand therefore, having your loins gird about with truth, and having on the breastplate of righteousness; [15] And your feet shod with the preparation of the gospel of peace; [16] Above all, taking the shield of faith, wherewith ye shall be able to quench all the fiery darts of the wicked. [17] And take the helmet of salvation, and the sword of the spirit, which is the word of God: [18] Praying always with all prayer and supplication in the Spirit, and watching thereunto with all perseverance and supplication for all saints.

God has equipped us with all we need to fight the good fight of faith. We have this supernatural armour. We have His Spirit living in us and He gives us authority over Satan and his demons. But we have to wrap all that He has given us in faith and prayer. Especially remember to take up the shield of faith. *Without faith it is impossible to please God* (Hebrews 11:6 KJV) Without faith, we cannot even get saved. It is by grace, through faith that we are saved, *it is the gift of God* (Ephesians 2:8) and not of our own doing.

We have God's Word *that never will return to Him void, but will accomplish that which He pleases and will do all that He has sent it out to do* (Isaiah 55:11). We have Jesus Who defeated the enemy on The Cross for our sakes so we can have eternal life. We have ministering and warring angels to protect and fight for us. We have many more promises from God that we can find in His Word.

Let's dig a little deeper into the armour of God, our supernatural protection to fight both offensively (attacking) and defensively (protecting). I like to tighten it up each day during my, and my husband's, daily devotions. We never take off our armour, but we reinforce it daily by remembering it, declaring it, and praying it over ourselves again and again.

The Belt of Truth, verse 14 (KJV) says it this way; *having your loins gird about with truth*. Other versions call it The Belt of Truth, which is my preference. The definition of the biblical girt is to gird, surround (King James Version Dictionary). To bind or encircle (Dictionary.com). We can assume that the Belt of truth would hold God's truth in place for us. Jesus said, "*And* *ye shall know the truth, and the truth shall make you free* (John 8:32 KJV)."

The Breastplate of Righteousness (verse 14, KJV). A breastplate is the part of armour that protects our hearts. In the physical sense, but also in the spiritual sense. We need our hearts to be protected from the lies of the enemy. From all his attacks. We need to keep a soft heart towards God so He can continue to mold us. Sometimes the enemy uses his lies to harden our hearts against God. Keep your righteousness (through the blood of Jesus) intact. Without Jesus, *our righteousness is as filthy rags* (Isaiah 64:6 KJV).

And Your Feet Shod with the Preparation of the Gospel of Peace (verse 15, KJV). We can take God's peace with us wherever we go. Ask God to gift you with His peace that passes all understanding, for you and for others. When you speak, people will feel the peace. Your voice can have a calming effect on others when God sends His spirit of peace flowing through you. I have experienced this in my own life.

Someone once told me, "Carla, I don't know why, but every time I talk to you it feels like all of my problems disappear." That's God!

Above all, taking **The Shield of Faith,** wherewith ye shall be able to quench all the fiery darts of the wicked (verse 16, KJV). Above all. Above all! Remember that. Above all, take up your shield of faith. Faith is so powerful in our spiritual warfare. Faith allows us to receive salvation. Faith helps us to refuse to believe the enemy's lies. Faith helps us to win this war. Whose report will you believe? I will believe the report of The Lord. I look forward to that day when I believe I will hear God say to me, *"You have fought the good fight of faith, enter in my good and faithful servant* (paraphrased Matthew 25:4 & 1 Timothy 6:12)." For more understanding on faith, please read over chapter 1.

And take **The Helmet of Salvation** (verse 17 (a) KJV). We receive this part of our armour when we get saved. A helmet protects our head. Our mind. When we get saved, we then can put on the mind of Christ, which changes our thinking. It can even change our reactions. It helps us make Godly decisions.

These things help to protect your body, soul, and spirit.

The Sword of the Spirit, which is The Word of God (verse 17 (b) KJV). We use our sword to defeat the enemy. Just as Jesus did in His example to us when tempted by Satan in the wilderness after fasting 40 days and nights. Satan knew that because Jesus was hungry and tired, he could take advantage of that weak area. Satan uses the same tactics on each of us. Wherever we are weakest, he attacks. The devil will try to take advantage when we are hungry, thirsty, tired, angry, or sick. These are just some of his tactics. We have to be on guard at all times. Even when we feel weak, God's word is mighty!

We can defeat the enemy of our souls, the devil, and his demons by wielding our sword, the bible. We have to actually use God's word. Just as a sword sitting on a shelf will never help you win a war, the same is with the bible if you don't use it, i.e., quote it, read it, read it out loud, memorize scriptures so you can use them at any given time. *Hide God's word in your heart that you may avoid sinning against Him* (read Psalm 119:11).

This armour God has given us is to protect us and to help us fight and win all the spiritual battles we encounter. We may still get knocked down from time to time, but we can get right back up and continue the fight of faith! We may get weak now and then, but it does not mean we are defeated. We hold on to God and His promises. We never let go. No matter what! If we need to take a break and rest—rest. But, as God spoke to me one time, *"Don't stay at the oasis too long."*

The glory of The Lord is our reward. He protects our back. He is on our right side and our left side. He goes before us. God is a refuge for us (Psalm 62:8 KJV). *He is our shield and buckler* (Psalm 91:4 KJV). Jesus is our example. Check out in Matthew chapter 4 how the devil tempted Him after He had been fasting for 40 days and nights. Jesus wielded The Sword of The Spirit (The Word of God), defeated the devil, and Satan left Him. Angels then came to minister to Him.

End of chapter thoughts: How can we use Christ's example to fight the *fight of faith*, use our armour, and defeat the enemy on our own behalf?

INSIGHT

CHAPTER THREE
Spiritual Warfare-Defeating The Enemy

It all begins with salvation. Once we give our hearts to Jesus, the mighty Spirit of God enters us. The bible says, "*greater is He that is in me than he that is in the world!*" (John 4:4) The Holy Spirit, the same spirit and power that rose Jesus from the dead, lives inside of me! If you have received Jesus as your personal Lord and Savior, then the same is true for you. Just think, at the name of Jesus demons tremble! What a wonderfully powerful name—Jesus!

On the other hand, the devil is nothing more than a liar, and the father of them. That means he created lying. The bible states that *Satan comes only to steal, and to kill, and to destroy* (John 10:10). This chapter is to help us understand better how to recognize his lies and tactics when he, and his demons, come at us. The bible, in Ephesians 6 verse 11, refers to these tactics as the "wiles" of the enemy. It means his tricks, deceits, lies, etc.

These are some of the weapons he uses against us. Every fiery dart he throws at us, he uses to provoke our emotions. We will have a variety of emotions, but we cannot allow our emotions to lead us. We will need to practice self-control (a fruit of the

Spirit).

Other tactics of the enemy include but, are not limited to, assigning the spirits of fear, hate, greed, condemnation, and temptations to sin (which is to distract and draw us away from God) because sin separates us from God. Isaiah 59:2 KJV says, *"But your iniquities have separated between you and your God and your sins have hid His face from you, that He will not hear."* That is why God sent Jesus, to be the ultimate sacrifice so we could be restored back to God. We then have open communication with our God.

The enemy will try to cause you to fall into sin and then use that very sin to bring condemnation and accusations against you to God. Once that happens and if you remain in that sin, you may begin to feel like a hypocrite and begin to walk away from God. But remember, in the 8th chapter and 1st verse of Romans (KJV) it says, *"There is therefore now no condemnation to them who are in Christ Jesus, who walk not after the flesh, but after the Spirit.*

Stay in Jesus. He is your Salvation. Satan is the accuser of men and *accuses us both day and night to our Father, God* (Revelation 12:10). The bible says in 1 Corinthians 10:13, *"There hath no temptation taken you but such as is common to man; but God is faithful Who will not suffer (allow) you to be tempted above that ye are able; (to bear) but will with the temptation, also make a way to escape, that ye may be able to bear it."*

God will provide a way out. The way out? The Word of God

says to be able to avoid temptation, don't go near it, do not look at it, do not go past it. In other words, run in the opposite direction! Don't contemplate it. Don't dwell on it. Change your thinking. You have to choose to do that. Get your mind back on Godly things. Stay focused on God's word.

In Philippians 4:8, it tells us to think on these things; *"Things that are true, honest, just, pure, lovely, of a good report "if there be any virtue and if there be any praise, think on these things."*

I have had to stand on The Word of God many times in order to stand strong in adversity. I wasn't always successful in the beginning, but as I stood it got easier because I got stronger in The Lord. When you have done all you can to stand, stand therefore (Ephesians 6:13-14).

As I move on with recognizing the enemy's voice, I want to share a personal testimony of mine because we need to be aware that the enemy will try to use our voices to speak his will to others. It's true. If you have ever spoken a rude or discouraging word to anyone, then you have personal experience with this. As Christians we wouldn't purposely choose to allow the enemy to use us against our brothers and sisters in The Lord, or against our loved ones, but at times, most, if not all, of us have.

I was working in a Christian School. All of the staff there were Christians. When I came into that workplace, The Lord began using me to help bring some spiritual insight and spiritual maturity to some of my co-workers. Most of these also became my friends. I had been working there for approximately 5 years and had spoken much about The Lord. I also, like in this chapter, spoke on recognizing and defeating the enemy. Two of my favorite things to do!

One day, the preschool director approached me and said, "Carla, I know this is a Christian school, but maybe you talk a little too much about Jesus."

I immediately knew where that was coming from. I thought, "Oh devil, I will not stop talking about Jesus!"

Then she went on to say, "And especially don't talk about the devil, that makes people uncomfortable."

You know who was really uncomfortable? The devil and his demons! I didn't reply to the director out of respect, but I told The Lord, "I will not be quiet unless YOU tell me to, Lord!" It was so obvious to me that the enemy was using this Christian woman's voice to speak what he wanted to say to me. She had no clue. She was in the flesh and not discerning the spiritual aspects.

I went to all of my co-workers and friends and asked them if I had ever made them uncomfortable talking about Jesus or the enemy. It was a resounding, "No way!"

When I left there a couple of years later, there were friends that asked me, "What are we going to do without you?" because The Lord had used me as a spiritual leader, encourager, and mentor there. They continued to go forward in The Lord and many of us remain friends today, many years later.

We should all realize that our soul is the enemy's target. That is our mind, will, and emotions. That is his playground. He works planting thoughts in our mind, trying to influence our decisions. If we allow those thoughts to take root (instead of casting them down) we will ultimately start making bad decisions and choices because of dwelling on them. This will in turn affect our emotions. Our emotions can get us into all kinds of troubles.

The Lord spoke to me during a very hard time in my life and said, *"Do not let your emotions lead you."* It made so much sense to me then and still does now. Of course it would! It came straight from The Holy Spirit!

My husband, Pastor Richard, always says, "The quality of our choices determines the quality of our lives." Think on that. Have you found that to be true? I know I most definitely have.

I think a good biblical example of how our choices determine the quality of our lives is found in Exodus. The story of when Moses led the Israelites through the wilderness after God uses him to set them free from the enslavement of the Egyptians. God had done many miraculous deeds in their sight, including the parting of the Red Sea to escape their enemies.

Even after all God did to rescue them, they murmured and complained against God whenever things got hard. Instead of praying to God and praising Him for all He had already done, all they did was complain. They even stooped so low as to make a golden calf to worship, instead of God! Their choices caused them to wander in the wilderness for 40 years. Just going around in circles. They had been on their way to the promised land, which was to take just days, but instead it took 40 years.

There are so many promises in the bible that the enemy wants to keep us from. He gives us all kinds of reasons to murmur and complain. But what we need to do to defeat the enemy in this area is to praise God through all circumstances. We don't have to praise Him "for" the hard times that we are going through, but praise Him just because of who He is. Praise Him for what He has already done. Praise Him for what He is going to do. Praise Him because He is more than worthy.

There have been many times when I have prayed, "Lord, I don't understand why this is going on, but I praise You; Lord, I don't like what is going on but, I love You; Lord, I'm not comfortable with this, but I serve you; Lord, I trust You!" I will believe the report of the Lord! It hasn't always been easy, but I know that God has all the answers, and I don't. And so, I continue forward in Him. Ultimately, I want to keep my relationship with Him strong and make it to heaven.

So how do we as Christians go about defeating the enemy of our soul? Through spiritual warfare. In Ephesians chapter 6, verses 10-18, it tells us to, *"Be strong and to put on the whole armour of God."* Let's read it again, starting in verse 10:

> [10] Finally, my brethren, be strong in The Lord, and in the power of His might. [11] Put on the whole armour of God, that

ye may be able to stand against the wiles of the devil. ¹² For we wrestle not against flesh and blood, but against Principalities, against powers, against the rulers of the darkness of this world, against spiritual wickedness in high places.

¹³ Wherefore take unto you the whole armour of God, that ye may be able to withstand in the evil day, and having done all, to stand. ¹⁴ Stand therefore, having your loins gird about with truth, and having on the breastplate of righteousness; ¹⁵and your feet shod with the preparation of the gospel of peace; ¹⁶ above all, taking the shield of faith, wherewith ye shall be able to quench all the fiery darts of the wicked. ¹⁷ And take the helmet of salvation, and the sword of the spirit, which is the word of God.

¹⁸ Praying always, with all prayer and supplication in the spirit, and watching thereunto with all perseverance and supplication for all saints.

I typed out this entire passage again because I want to make sure you know it. It is a very crucial part of our living a victorious life here on earth, while we watch and wait for the coming of our Lord, Jesus Christ. God has given us His word for our instruction. If we want to do it right, that is, build a godly life, then we need to read the instructions. Have you seen this Acronym—B.I.B.L.E?—Basic Instructions Before Leaving Earth. I'm not sure where I first saw this, but I like it.

As we study how to defeat the enemy and his demons, I would like to go more into depth on the armour of God. This will help as you study it, learn it, and memorize it (which I strongly advise). This armour is your defense against Satan and his demons, and through faith it works! Notice that the shield of faith is part of our armour and that The Word says to *"Especially take up the shield of faith."*

Why is our faith so important? As a reminder, and first of all, we are saved by grace, through faith; Ephesians 2:8, *For by grace are ye saved through faith; and that not of yourselves: it is the gift of God.* Second, we cannot please God without faith; Hebrews 11:6, *But without faith it is impossible to please Him: for he that cometh to God must believe that He is, and that He is a rewarder of them that diligently seek Him.*

Thankfully, The Lord says that *He has given a measure of faith to everyone* (Romans 12:3 (b) KJV). We are to *walk by faith, not by sight* (2 Corinthians 5:7). We must *fight the good fight of faith* (1 Timothy 6:12). *Faith without works is dead* (James 2:26), and so on. There are many scriptures concerning faith.

Anyone who wants to spend eternity with God must first believe that He is. That takes faith. (See chapter 1 for more details on faith)

Now, let's think about how we are able to use our armour to defeat the enemy. Start with the helmet of salvation and the hope of salvation for others. Without salvation, we have no weapons against demonic forces. We first are to put on that helmet of salvation through Jesus, our Messiah, the Son of God. We do that by asking Him to forgive us of all our sins and to come into our lives and to be our Lord and Savior.

Now, we have The Holy Spirit living inside of us and *greater is He (God) that lives within us than he (the enemy) that lives in the world* (1 John 4:4-5). We must guard our minds. Philippians 4:7 says, *"And the peace of God, which surpasseth all understanding, shall keep your hearts and minds through Christ Jesus."* In Philippians 4:8 *it tells us to think on these things: things that are true, honest, just, pure, lovely and things that are of a good report.*

We also have the Breastplate of Righteousness, which protects our hearts from all the lies that the demons tell us. We may hear them, but they don't have to penetrate our hearts.

Next is the belt of truth. What does a belt do? It holds our armour on. What is this supernatural belt? Truth! The Bible says that the Truth (Jesus) will set us free. Jesus saith unto him, *I am the Way, the Truth, and the Life, no one comes to the Father but by me* (John 14:6).

As I am going down the list of our armour, we come to our feet. They have shoes of peace on. We can have God's *peace that surpasses all understanding!* (Philippians 4:7) We can take that peace everywhere we go.

We also have our Sword of the Spirit, our Bible, The Word of God! This sword slices and dices the enemy. How? By using God's Word (each scripture) to combat the lies of the devil and his demons.

When they tell you a lie or try to cause fear or anything else that is against God's word, we can speak God's word out of our mouth, and it is like a two-edged sword. I'd like to give some examples on how to use God's Word, our sword, to defeat the enemy. We will begin with Jesus' example to us. In Matthew chapter 4, beginning with verse 1, after Jesus had been fasting for 40 days and nights, the bible says that He was approached by the devil who began to tempt Him.

Jesus used scripture to combat the enemy. Jesus, of course, was hungry, and the devil says to Him, "If Thou be The Son of God, command that these stones be made bread."

Jesus answered and said, *"It is written, man shall not live by bread alone, but by every word that proceedeth out of the mouth of God."*

Then the devil went on to tempt Jesus further, even trying to use the scriptures against Him. But Jesus replied, *"It is written again, thou shalt not tempt the Lord thy God."*

Jesus only used scripture to defeat the enemy's temptations. Jesus finally told him, *"Get thee hence Satan!"* Satan then left Him. They were spiritually having a sword fight. We have authority to do the same.

Continuing on with our armour, the bible says to *especially take up your shield of faith which quenches all the fiery darts of the enemy.* Shield of faith, activate! Keep your faith active. Be on guard at all times. *Faith without works is dead* (James 2:26).

If we lay down our shield, it isn't any help to us is it? If we lay down our sword, how can we fight? If we don't have on our helmet, we can't protect our minds, can we? We need to put on our armour, through prayer, and keep it on each day, also through prayer. Remember, praise ambushes the enemy! Put on the garment of praise for the spirit of heaviness! Isaiah 61:3 It works!

Another powerful weapon apart from the armour of God is the combination of prayer and fasting. Prayer definitely will move God's hand, but sometimes we need to add fasting to our prayers. Especially for deliverances. In Mark chapter 9, it tells how Jesus rebuked a foul spirit and caused it to come out and leave a man's son.

Afterward, the Disciples went to Him privately and asked Him why they were not able to cast the demon out. In verse 29 of that same chapter, Jesus said to them; "this kind can come forth by nothing, but by prayer and fasting". In Isaiah 58, The Lord speaks of the type of fasting that He has chosen for us to do.

A few other ways we can defeat the enemy is by interceding for others, through giving thanksgiving and praise to God for all He has done, is doing, and will do. Also, by the word of our testimony and by pleading the blood of the Lamb. In Revelation 12:11 it says, *"And they overcame him (Satan) by the blood of the Lamb, and by the word of their testimony, and they loved not their lives unto death."*

Another powerful way to be victorious over the enemy is to pray in the Spirit. If you have been baptized in the Holy Ghost with the evidence of speaking in tongues, I would use this gift of the Spirit as much as you are able. Although I speak in tongues pretty often, I still need to improve in this area myself. God has given us gifts, tools, and weapons to use against the tricks and attacks of the enemy. We need to be sure to be aware of them and learn to utilize them.

God loves us, and He wants us to live in victory. These spiritual weapons make all the difference in our battle against Satan and his demons. Ephesians 6:12 reminds us, *"For we wrestle not against flesh and blood but against spiritual wickedness."* Also, 2 Corinthians 10:3-4 says, *"For though we walk in the flesh, we do not war after the flesh: for the weapons of our warfare are not carnal, but mighty through God to the pulling down of strongholds."*

I would also like to remind you of some scriptures which help us to defeat the devil and his lying demons. Beginning with Ephesians 6:11, *Put on the whole armour of God that ye may be able to stand against the wiles of the devil.*

2 Timothy 1:7, *God has not given us the spirit of fear but of power and of love and of a sound mind.*

Romans 8:1, *There is therefore now no condemnation to them which are in Christ Jesus, who walk not after the flesh, but after the Spirit.*

1 Corinthians 10:13, *There hath no temptation taken you but such as is common to man: but God is faithful, Who will not suffer you to be tempted above that ye are able; but will with*

the temptation also make a way of escape that ye may be able to bear it.

Matthew 26:41, *Watch and pray that ye enter not into temptation: the spirit indeed is willing, but the flesh is weak.*

We also need to remember to protect our minds. 2 Corinthians 10:5 says to, *cast down imaginations and every high thing that exalteth itself against the knowledge of God, and bringing into captivity every thought to the obedience of Christ.*

Also, Philippians 4:6-7, *Be careful for nothing; but in everything by prayer and supplication with thanksgiving let your requests be made known unto God. And the peace of God, which passeth all understanding, shall keep your hearts and minds through Christ Jesus.*

Philippians 4:9, *Those things which ye have both learned and received, and heard and seen in Me, do: and the God of peace shall be with you.*

Another way to protect our minds is by being cautious in what we are watching and listening to. If the quote "Trash in, trash out" is true, then so is "God in, God out."

Remember to think on good things. Anoint your home. Obey God's word. Be faithful to Him, for He is The Faithful One! Take time to spend quality, one-on-one time with Him. Stay heavenly minded, not focusing on the things of this world. Look up for your redemption, draweth nigh.

Now to close out this chapter, I want to share one of my

favorite verses concerning Satan; Isaiah 14:16, *"Those that see you will gaze upon you and consider you saying: Is this the man that made the earth to tremble?"* I love this verse because it exposes Satan for what he really is.

But unless we call on The Holy Spirit and the authority God has given us over Satan and his demons, we will not be able to defeat him on all sides. This is always a spiritual battle, never a physical or emotional one.

On the other hand, acknowledging how great and powerful our God is and remembering that *greater is He that is in us than he that is in the world*, can make all the difference in defeating this foe.

End of Chapter Thoughts: There are so many areas that the enemy tries to deceive us. He will try anything he can to get us to give up. But if we give up, what are we really accomplishing? What are some ways you can be sure to defeat the enemy in your own life? How can you help others fight their spiritual battles?

CHAPTER FOUR
Prayer | Intercession | Fasting

Prayer, by definition, is a solemn request for help or expression of thanks addressed to God or an object of worship (Oxford Languages Dictionary). Well, I can tell you right now, my prayers go to God, The Father, The Creator of heaven and earth, and never to an "object" of worship. If you want your prayers to be heard, I suggest the same for you. An object of worship, whether an inanimate object or a mere human, cannot hear or answer your prayers.

There is a passage in the Old Testament book of 1 Kings 18: 21-39 that I love to read and share with others. This passage is of Elijah's testing of Baal. There were 450 prophets of Baal and only 1 prophet of God, Elijah. In verse 21, Elijah asks, *"How long halt ye between two opinions? If the Lord be God, then follow Him: but if Baal, then follow him."*

Elijah was pretty much saying, make up your mind. No one answered him. Then Elijah put out a challenge. A test between the god Baal and The Lord God. So, Elijah told the people to gather two bullocks. One for them to get ready for a burnt sacrifice to Baal and one for him to get ready for a sacrifice to The Lord. He also told them to lay it on wood, but not to put any fire under the sacrifice, and he would do the same. Then Elijah said, *"Call on the name of your gods and I will call on the name of the Lord, and the God that answers by fire, let Him be God."*

All the people agreed, and they took their bullock and prepared it and began to call on their god, Baal. They called on their god from morning till noon with no answer, and they began to get angry and jumped on the altar they had made.

About that time, Elijah began to mock them, saying things like, *"Cry aloud, for he is a god. Either he is talking or pursuing or on a journey. Maybe he is sleeping and needs to be awakened. Cry out louder to him."*

Then the people began to cry louder to Baal and also began to cut themselves until their blood gushed out. They called on their god until evening with no response.

Finally, Elijah took 12 stones and built an altar in the name of The Lord. He then dug a trench around it and had the wood and the bullock placed on the altar. He then had 4 barrels of water poured out on the bullock and the wood. He instructed the people to do that a second and a third time. The water ran all over the sacrifice and overflowed, and water was poured into the trenches around the altar. Elijah looked up to heaven and in verse 37 (a) said, hear me oh Lord, hear me that these people may know that Thou art the Lord God. Then the fire of the Lord fell (verse 38) and consumed the burnt sacrifice, the wood, the stones, the dust, and licked up the water that was in the trench! And when all the people saw it (verse 39), they fell on their faces: and they said, the Lord, He is the God; the Lord, He is the God.

What a mighty God we serve! He is the one and only true and living God. The only one capable of hearing and answering our prayers. Don't be deceived, He hears and will answer in His perfect timing if we are not praying amiss (inappropriately) and we believe. Matthew 21:22 says *when we pray without doubting, we shall receive what we ask for*.

It sounds like Elijah believed. And what a sight to see! That would make most people believe that *"The Lord, He is God!"* If you would like, you can go to the 18th chapter of 1 Kings and read for yourself all the details about Elijah challenging the prophets of Baal and how God was faithful to answer.

Besides prayer being, as defined, a request or thanksgiving made to God, prayer is simply communication with God. Before we accept Jesus Christ as our Lord and Savior, we are God's creation. Once we accept Him, we are given the right to become God's child. It says in His word that *God does not hear a sinner's prayer* (John 9:31 KJV) because sin separates us from God. That is, until we ask His Son Jesus to forgive us of all our sins and His blood cleanses us from all sin and unrighteousness. Once we ask for forgiveness and accept Jesus into our hearts, this opens up communication for us with God, The Father. *We now can go boldly to His throne* (Hebrews 4:16 KJV). *We are no longer sinners but have become the righteousness of God* (2 Corinthians 5:21).

This does not mean we won't sin, but we have an advocate,

Jesus, who forgives us as soon as we ask. We can now pray to God about anything that we desire. Anything concerning you or others, or just to talk to Him. But especially to give Him praise and to worship Him. Talk to God—The Father, God—The Son, and God—The Holy Spirit, as much as you would like. The more, the better.

There is another way available for God's children to pray. That is in The Holy Ghost, also called speaking in tongues. This gift of prayer comes through the baptism of The Holy Ghost. If you have received this gift with the evidence of speaking in tongues, this is a prayer that comes with power by the Holy Ghost. It is actually The Holy Spirit (Holy Ghost) interceding for us and for others through us. This kind of prayer can also be used when you don't know how or what to pray.

Along with this gift sometimes comes the gift of interpretation, so the Church can be edified. The one with this gift, The Lord gives interpretation of the tongues in their known language so they can give a word of encouragement from The Lord.

Intercession by definition is the action of saying a prayer on behalf of another person (Oxford Languages Dictionary). We are called to pray for others and to stand in the gap on their behalf. In 1 Timothy 2:1 KJV it says, *"I exhort therefore, that, first of all, supplications, prayers, intercessions, and giving of thanks, be made for all men."*

There are also scriptures that tell us that Jesus intercedes for us. Romans 8:34 (b) KJV says, *"It is Christ that died, yea rather, that is risen again, Who is even at the right hand of God, Who also maketh intercession for us.*" Isn't that something—to know that Jesus is praying to The Father for us?

Fasting by definition is to abstain from all or some kinds of food or drink, especially as a religious observance (Oxford Languages Dictionary). Fasting is a very powerful addition to prayer and intercession.

Fasting is to set the captive free. In Isaiah 58:6 KJV it says, "*Is not this the fast that I have chosen? To loose the bands of wickedness, to undo the heavy burdens, and to let the oppressed go free, and that ye break every yoke?*"

In Mark chapter 9, the disciples tried to cast demons out and could not. When they asked Jesus why, He answered and said *this kind can come forth by nothing, but by prayer and fasting* (Mark 9:29 KJV). Fasting gives more supernatural power to our prayers. It helps to get the desired answer to our prayers when there is spiritual warfare going on.

I have experienced the differences spiritual fasting can make. But when you fast, be sure to do it privately between you and The Lord. What you do in private, God will reward openly. Be sure that when you fast, others cannot tell by your conduct or the look on your face. And if you seek the recognition of people, that is the only reward you will receive.

It is okay to go on a fast with others, but be the best example to them that you can be. In my opinion, I think it is okay to let someone know that you will be or have fasted for them and their needs, but only to encourage them and make them feel supported.

Prayer, intercession, and fasting move the hand of God, but especially when they are done in faith. Sometimes the answer seems slow in coming, but don't give up. God has a perfect plan, and He has perfect timing. Trust Him. Proverbs 3:5,6 KJV says to, *"Trust in the Lord with all thine heart; and lean not unto thine own understanding. In all thy ways acknowledge Him, and He shall direct thy paths."* Jesus even told His disciples to *trust God.*

God's ways are far above our ways and His thoughts far above our thoughts. I will not put my trust in any man, but I will trust in my God. I will pray and wait. Isaiah 40:31 (a) KJV says; *"But they that wait on the Lord shall renew their strength."*

End of Chapter Thoughts: Do you have anyone or anything on your heart that you could intercede and fast for?

CHAPTER FIVE
Sacrifice & Obedience

Let us first look at some biblical definitions of sacrifice and obedience, and then we will look in God's word to see what He has to say about them.

Beginning with sacrifice, the Easton's Bible Dictionary says that the offering up of sacrifices is to be regarded as a divine institution.

It did not originate with man. God Himself appointed it as the mode in which acceptable worship was to be offered to Him by a guilty man (we are born into sin). This was how it was to be, at least until the only perfect and holy sacrifice, Christ Jesus, died on the cross as the ultimate sacrifice for mankind.

Nailed on that cross with Jesus were all our sins. Once and for all. We only need to accept Jesus' sacrifice, ask Him to forgive us of all our sins, and invite Him into our lives as our Lord and Savior. We then become a child of God, saved and sanctified.

Most of us know John 3:16 KJV which states, *"For God so loved the world that He gave His only begotten Son, that whosoever believeth in Him should not perish but have*

INSIGHT

everlasting life."

John 3:17 KJV goes on to say, *"For God sent not His Son into the world to condemn the world, but that the world through Him might be saved."*

As I said, Jesus was the ultimate sacrifice for the sins of the world. There is no need for anyone to continue to sacrifice animals that only temporarily cover their sins. Jesus' blood does not just cover our sins but washes our sins away. His blood cleanses us as if we never had them to begin with. What a miracle we have through Him!

Of course, there are other types of sacrifices. We can *bring a sacrifice of praise to God* (Hebrews 13:15 KJV). Giving praise to God is easy when everything is going well. We praise Him for all He has done. We praise Him because He is good to us. But what about when things are not going so well? Our faith will surely be put to the test. That is when a "sacrifice" of praise is sometimes necessary.

It reminds me of the Israelites, when God delivered them out of bondage from Egypt (Exodus 13:14). Instead of praising God for all He had done, they only murmured and complained when things didn't go smoothly. Because they did not offer up a sacrifice of praise to God, but instead made and worshipped a golden calf, it took them 40 years of wandering in the wilderness before they reached their promise. Many of them died before reaching that land flowing with milk and honey. Many of them died before receiving that promise because of their disobedience to God. Because of rebelliousness. Because of sin. If they had praised God in the hard times, as well as the good and miraculous times, it would only have taken them eleven days to reach the promised land. They all would have made it.

We need to be sure to praise God (just for Who He is) at all times if we want to continue to go forward and be able to obtain our promises sooner rather than later. Although sacrifice is very important to God, it says in His Word *that obedience is even better than sacrifice* (1 Samuel 15:22 KJV).

Being obedient to God and His word will bring about many blessings to your life. It will cause many difficulties to bypass you. That doesn't mean you won't have your share of troubles, but *God will bring you out of them all* (Psalm 34:17 KJV). God loves obedience. I would advise that you do your best to obey Him, even when it is challenging to do so. He knows your future. You will reap the benefits. Will He find you faithful?

Sometimes it takes a sacrifice to sow (give). Since we reap what we sow, it is more blessed to sow largely, but if you sow (or plant) sparingly, you will receive sparingly. 2 Corinthians 9:6 KJV says it this way, *"But this I say, he which soweth sparingly shall reap also sparingly; and he which soweth bountifully shall reap also bountifully."* This sure speaks to me.

The Bible says to give even out of your own need. God is looking at our hearts. He loves a cheerful giver. In 2 Corinthians 9:7 KJV it goes on to say, *"Every man according as he purposeth in his heart, so let him give; not grudgingly, or of necessity: for God loveth a cheerful giver."*

INSIGHT

It definitely is a sacrifice for most of us when we give of our finances, especially when we may have a need of our own. This makes me think of the poor widow who gave all she had. It was only 2 mites (less than a penny these days) but it may have paid for some need she had. The wealthy may have given thousands, but she gave more than them all. She had nothing left. They still had overflow. If they would have taken all that they had and gave it, then they would have given as much as the widow woman did. See Mark 12:32 KJV.

We can also give of our time, talents, resources, etc. Sowing does not always mean financial, although it does many times. God's word tells us in Malachi chapter 3, verses 8-11 KJV, *to bring all your tithes and offerings to the storehouse.* I believe in this day and time that would be your church, or if you don't attend a church, wherever you are fed spiritually (not attending a church does not exempt us from giving tithes and offerings to The Lord). And remember, we are to give from our first fruits, our gross amount—not net.

This would fall under the heading of obedience. In verse 8 God says *we have robbed Him* and verse 9 says that *we have brought a curse upon ourselves.* How have we robbed God? In tithes and offerings (also verse 8). It is better to be obedient to God. If you did not have this understanding before, you can remedy it now.

This is a good place to share how God helped me some years ago, to push through and pay my tithes when I was hesitant to let the finances go. I had been paying tithes faithfully for some time. All of a sudden, my finances took a plunge, and I realized that the exact amount of tithes I had been paying was the exact amount that I had just lost. Out of fear (because I was looking at my budget), I was holding on tight to that 10%.

Well, of course the first thing I thought was "that's my tithes!" (obviously, I needed some spiritual growth in this area). A better reaction might have been, that's my gas money, or grocery money, etc. Because this was a spiritual test, the tithes came to mind first. At the time, if I had been a more mature Christian, I could have had a better reaction like, God is faithful! He will provide. I need to continue to pay my tithes, first.

Well, as I went along, I would put into the offering plate only what I was comfortable to give. I would ask The Lord to forgive me and to help me to do better. I was under conviction. I was determined that I would come out of this test victoriously. I was not going to give up. I had to overcome the spirit of fear and doubt. I needed to use my faith and trust God. I needed to be obedient and give what I believed was required of me.

The insight God gave to me concerning "not" paying my tithes was this, "If someone gave me money to pass on to another person for them and I instead stuck it in my pocket, thinking, 'this is exactly the amount I need to buy my groceries this week, I can't give it to them. I need it!'"

What have I just done? I just stole someone else's money. I robbed them. Well, God has said that we rob Him when we do not give 10% back to Him. He allows us to keep 90%!

INSIGHT

Once I realized the 10% I was holding back was not mine, I made a decision. Since my budget was causing fear, I told God I wasn't going to look at my budget any longer. I was going to pay the 10% and believe He would make sure the 90% left over would be enough. I began walking by faith.

I did my part, and God did the rest. I haven't missed paying my tithes since. And I also remembered the freewill offering. God loves a cheerful giver (2 Corinthians 9:7 KJV)! So in this instance, I was able to become obedient and over time give sacrificially too. One thing I learned though, if you don't pay your tithes, that money most likely will end up going on car repairs or other financial emergencies. You might as well give to The Lord willingly, in obedience, and with a glad heart. It sure can become a huge blessing to you.

I don't remember how long it took, months at least, but one day God started giving me insight. When He revealed to me I was actually robbing Him just as the scripture states, it was like He told me a mini parable. If you haven't been paying tithes, it may stretch your faith to do so. Do it by faith in obedience to God's word. He will honor it. God says *prove Me now, if I won't open to you the windows of heaven and pour you out a blessing that there is not enough room to receive it* (Malachi 3:10 KJV paraphrased)

Prayer: Dear Lord, please forgive me for where I have not been obedient to You. Help me Lord to be an obedient follower of Yours. Help me to bring a sacrifice of praise to You. You are more than worthy, Lord.

In Jesus' Name, Amen!

End of Chapter Thoughts: What are ways that you can bring a sacrifice of praise to God? How can you better be obedient to His word?

INSIGHT

CHAPTER SIX
Spiritual Gifts

In 1 Corinthians chapter 12:1 KJV, Paul is writing and begins by saying, "*Now concerning spiritual gifts, brethren, I would not have you ignorant.*" It is a good thing to understand the gifts of the Spirit. They are for the edification (building up) of the church. That is why Paul instructs us *to especially desire to prophecy* (1 Corinthians 14 KJV).

The spiritual gifts that the bible speaks about are such a blessing to have. Especially if you are in ministry. The Holy Spirit gives to different people, different gifts. 1 Corinthians 12:4 KJV says this, "*Now there are diversities of gifts, but the same Spirit.*"

Some people in ministry even have multiple giftings. These gifts include the word of wisdom, the word of knowledge, faith, healings, the working of miracles, prophecy, discerning of spirits, divers kinds of tongues, and the interpretation of tongues (1 Corinthians 12:8-10 KJV). *But all these worketh that one and the selfsame Spirit* (1 Corinthians 12:11 (a) KJV).

God has appointed some in the church different jobs, as well as giftings. In verse 28 (a) of Corinthians chapter 12 KJV says,

"And God has set some in the church first apostles, secondarily prophets, thirdly teachers." Ephesians 4:11 says, *"[11] And He gave some, apostles; and some prophets; and some evangelists; and some pastors and teachers; [12] For the perfecting of the saints, for the work of the ministry, for the edifying of the body of Christ. We being the body of Christ and He the head* (1 Corinthians 11:3) & (Ephesians 5:23 KJV)."

Let's take a look at each gift individually. Although the first two are not clearly explained in the bible, I think most understanding on the gifts of the word of wisdom and the word of knowledge comes through experiencing them. These are a gift of "words" of wisdom or "words" of knowledge, not a "gift" of wisdom or knowledge (you don't become wiser or more knowledgeable in a general sense).

I believe that when The Lord has spoken "revelation knowledge" and then that insight is relayed to others, it could be a form of the word of wisdom or of knowledge. The Lord also will reveal unknown information to us (that only God could have revealed to us), to share with others when we have the gift of knowledge. Let's dig just a little deeper.

The Word of Wisdom (1 Corinthians 12:8 KJV) A supernatural utterance of things only God could know and wisdom to act accordingly. It can be used to instruct someone how to deal with a situation. It gives supernatural insight. Similar to the gift of prophecy, but not as intense or given in the diverse ways prophecy can be given. It is a verbal revelation or insight. I believe The Holy Spirit will fill the prophets' mouth with the message or information He wants to convey. The bottom line is that it is used to edify, encourage, and can help to build the church.

The Word of Knowledge (1 Corinthians 12:8 KJV) There is given a supernatural impression that reveals, encourages, or edifies the individual or church on the receiving end. Also, it is very similar to the gift of prophecy, but on a smaller scale. The one with the gift of knowledge is shown things that they couldn't know without The Holy Spirit revealing it to them. They are able to speak truths to individuals. For example, what areas in their body needs healing, or are being healed. Also, other areas in their lives that God is touching or will be. The gift of knowledge can be used to confirm information, God's calling on people's lives, etc.

The Gift of Faith (1 Corinthians 12:9 KJV) God has given us all a portion of faith (we are saved through faith), but the gift of faith is much more. It is supernatural, and those who have this gift can believe for what others perceive as impossible. The gift of faith can even cause the person who has it to seem as though they cannot face reality or that they are in denial as I mentioned in chapter one. Every spiritual gift from God is supernatural and is meant to be used in ministry for His glory. It makes standing on His promises in the bible much more attainable, but not without some ridicule, even from other believers. This gift, like all the others, is to edify and build up the church.

The Gift of Healings (1 Corinthians 12:9 KJV) As you may notice, this gifting is plural—healings. I believe this is because we not only have a need for physical healings but also for emotional and spiritual healings. Physical healing is the one most people think of when they hear the term "healing." Emotional healing could include broken hearts, depression, sadness, etc. Spiritual healing would include being set free from spiritual attacks. I also would call this deliverance. All kinds of healing tend to be accompanied with the gift of faith.

At the moment of prayer, it is God's choice whether He heals the individual or not. Some healings, miracles, etc. come later. That is why we should never give up. Sometimes He does not heal here, but instead, when the individual passes from here to eternity with The Lord; they are most definitely healed there.

I have personally experienced receiving healing in my body. I have also seen and heard of healing in others who were prayed for. From back pain to cancer. God is able! My gift in this area is more geared towards deliverance. I have experienced many deliverances from depression, oppression and right out attacks from the enemy. Even for myself. Praise God!

The Working of Miracles (1 Corinthians 12:10 KJV) As with the gift of healing, the working of miracles tend to be accompanied with the gift of faith. Miracles are supernatural manifestations that only God can do or allow. They are humanly impossible, although God will work miracles through His servants. The working of miracles is one of the most powerful ways for God to prove Himself God. He did so many miracles through Jesus that it caused people to believe and be saved. God wants to bless His children through miracles as well as through other means, but salvation is the ultimate goal. He can accomplish this through His supernatural signs, wonders, and miracles.

The Gift of Prophecy (1 Corinthians 12:10 KJV) The Bible tells us t*o especially desire to prophesy*. Prophecy is divine insight given through the prophet to the church, by The Holy Spirit. It tells of future events, revealed to the prophet either through dreams, visions, direct communication from an angel of God, or The Holy Spirit Himself. *Prophecy is for edification, exhortation, and comfort* (1 Corinthians 14:3 KJV).

Discerning of Spirits (1 Corinthians 12:10 KJV) The gift of discerning of spirits allows us to know the difference between a good spirit or an evil spirit. It seems that this would be obvious, but since the enemy can come in as a *"wolf in sheep's clothing,"* it may not be. The enemy can also appear *"as an angel of light"* (2 Corinthians 11:14 KJV). In 1 John 4:1 (a) KJV it says, *"Beloved, believe not every spirit, but try the spirits if they are of God."* Another way to say this is to "test" the spirits to see if they are from God. We need to pray for this gift to flow in our lives so we can more readily avoid being deceived by demonic spirits.

Divers Kinds of Tongues (1 Corinthians 12:10 KJV) "Divers" means diverse. Tongues means languages. This is another of the gifts of The Holy Spirit, also called the Baptism of the Holy Ghost (or Spirit) with the "evidence" of speaking in tongues. As I said, this is a "gift" of The Holy Spirit in the same manner as all the other gifts are given. This gift is not a prerequisite to making it to heaven, as some teach. It is a gift.

INSIGHT

The Spirit of God gives these different gifts to individuals as He chooses. One type of tongues is when The Holy Spirit prays through an individual to God. It is their personal heavenly prayer language. They do not know what is being prayed. This gift of tongues is exceptional in that the Holy Ghost will pray through you as you utter this heavenly language. In 1 Corinthians 14:14-15 KJV it states, *"^{14} For if I pray in an unknown tongue, my spirit prayeth, but my understanding is unfruitful. ^{15} What is it then? I will pray with the spirit, and I will pray with the understanding also: I will sing with the spirit, and I will sing with the understanding also."*

This scripture gives us evidence that it is also possible to sing "in the spirit" and to interpret "in the spirit." I have experienced the singing in the spirit but not of the singing of the interpretation—yet! I look forward to that time. The evidence that a person has been baptized in The Holy Ghost "and with fire" (Matthew 3:11 KJV) can be a stammering of lips, an unknown tongue, or even tongues of other foreign languages that are not known to the individual speaking. The Lord uses the latter of the three when ministering in foreign countries where we don't know the language.

Interpretation of Tongues (1 Corinthians 12:10 KJV) Interpretation of tongues is also a gift of The Holy Spirit. It is used with one of the divers types of tongues so that the church may be edified. This is not the same as the personal prayer language that we initially receive. In my experience we cannot speak in this tongue at will, as we can with our personal heavenly prayer language. When interpreted, it is usually a direct word from God to the hearers in the language understood. A person with the gift of interpretation is prompted by The Holy Spirit to begin speaking out a word of interpretation, and then The Holy Spirit continues to flow like in what Psalm 45:1 (b) says, *"My tongue is the pen of a ready writer."*

I love that. Praise God!

End of Chapter Thoughts: Have you received any of these gifts? Are you actively using your gift (s)? Besides these gifts of the Spirit, what other kind of giftings does The Lord give to us? Do you flow in any of these? i.e., singing…

INSIGHT

CHAPTER SEVEN
The Fruit of The Spirit

What is the meaning of the fruit of the Spirit? These are the characteristics, values and morals that should become evident in our lives as we serve The Lord. Just as an apple tree should produce apples, a Christian should produce the fruit of The Spirit. And, just as it takes time for the apples to begin to bud and grow, so does the fruit of the Spirit in a Christian's life.

If you have been a Christian for a long time, you should have most, if not all, the fruit of the Spirit growing out of you. In Galatians 5:22-23 KJV the list is this, *"Love, joy, peace, longsuffering, gentleness, goodness, faith, meekness, and temperance."* Ephesians 5:9 says, *"For the fruit of the Spirit is in all goodness and righteousness and truth."*

Now, let us break each one down. The first one mentioned is **love**. That seems easy enough, right? Well, with God, it goes much deeper than loving those who love you. The bible says *we are to love even our enemies*. How can we do that? Only through God's love. *God is love* (1 John 4:8).

It doesn't mean we love what people say or do. It doesn't mean we even like anything about them. But it does mean we are to love their souls. We are to treat others with love. God's love. God even loved those who crucified His Son, Jesus. Jesus died for them as much as He died for you and me.

The bible tells us to love our neighbors as ourselves. What does that really mean? Well, we take care of ourselves. We go to the doctor if we are sick. We feed ourselves when we are hungry. We give ourselves something to drink when we are thirsty. We ask others to pray for us when we are in need. We make sure we have clothes to wear. We make friends to keep loneliness at bay and for support.

All these things, and more, we should do to show God's love to others. When we see a need that we can meet, we are to meet that need if possible, today! The Word of God says not to send them away saying come back tomorrow, but to meet their needs right then if it is in our power to do so. And be sure you are giving cheerfully, not expecting anything in return.

The Lord told me one time, "*I'm going to teach you to love the un-loveable.*" And so it began. He sent people to me that were very challenging to communicate with because of their "unlovely" ways. But I was able to stay focused on showing God's love to them. I was sharing this testimony to someone, and The Lord spoke to me at that moment and said, "*Yes, and I'm going to send more,*" and He has.

Everyone needs love. Be the one. In Luke 6:32 it asks *what thanks is there when you love those who love you? Even sinners love those who love them* (Paraphrased).

The second fruit of the Spirit mentioned is *joy*. The Word of God says that *the joy of the Lord is our strength* (Nehemiah 8:10 (b) KJV). Joy is not the same as happiness. It goes much deeper and can last forever. But watch out. The enemy likes to try to steal our joy if he can.

What is the difference between happiness and joy? Happiness is temporary. For example, celebrating a special occasion can make us happy. Going on a vacation can make us happy. Finding a new friend can make us happy. Buying a new car or a new home can make us happy. But just like they say, once the new wears off…

With the joy of The Lord, it is rooted in us. We may go through things that cause us not to feel that joy so strongly because of our emotions, but it can still be there inside. Have you ever met someone who was a Christian, strong, and always seemed to be smiling? Even through tough times? Of course, they will have their moments of sadness, anger, or even worry, but they always seem to bounce back quickly and completely. Maybe even better than they were before. I believe that is evidence of the joy of The Lord.

Third is *peace*. Oh, what a blessing! To have the peace of God that surpasses all understanding. Philippians 4:7 KJV says, *"And the peace of God, which passeth all understanding, shall keep your hearts and minds in Christ Jesus."* That is the best peace. The Lord said in John 14:27 KJV, *"Peace I leave with you. My peace I give unto you."*

From my experience, I found the most peace came through

my faith. Believing that God really is in control and that He will work all things out for my good. If you can believe that wholeheartedly, you will have peace. I remember how much better I felt when I went through a familiar past trial but had the peace of God. Even though the circumstances were the same, I had complete peace. It was an eye opener of how walking by faith can bring the peace of God. It revealed some insight into how our faith and trust in Jesus makes all the difference as we go through our trials. I just smiled to myself.

Next on the list, **longsuffering**. Simply defined, it means to have patience. What a blessing to know that our Heavenly Father is longsuffering with us. How many of us need this fruit to grow in us? Probably most, if not all of us could use some fertilizing in this area. But how do we accomplish that?

What kind of fertilizer? In James 1:2-3 KJV it says, "*My brethren, count it all joy when you fall into divers temptations; knowing this, that the trying of your faith worketh patience.*" I mention faith quite often in this book, but chapter 1 has a more in depth look at walking by faith.

Let's look at the next fruit, **gentleness**. I think gentleness is pretty easy to understand. Not just gentleness in our actions, but also in our words and attitude. By being gentle, that is kind, calm and could include being soft-spoken. In this way we may be able to help others be more comfortable with us. We can make friends.

We may even be better able to win souls with this fruit growing from us. Even frightened animals have been won over through gentleness. If you tend to be harsh and overbearing, then this is a place to pray over yourself. We are ambassadors of Christ and it is His reputation on the line, too.

Of the fruit of the Spirit, **goodness** is next. There is a lot that can be said on this topic. When we look to the Greek language to define goodness, it means an uprightness of heart and life. Spiritually, I believe it means more of how we treat others than just being "good." We can be a good person but still not be in right standing with God. We are not saved through works, but through the blood of Jesus. Then, after salvation, good works are expected from us and will be rewarded in heaven, and some even here. The reward is not our motivation, though. Pleasing God is.

One of the most powerful fruits of the Spirit, in my experience, is *faith*. Chapter 1 is completely dedicated to this fruit. Faith is so important to us as Christians, and for many reasons. First of all, *without faith, we cannot please God* (Hebrews 11:6). Secondly, *it is through faith, by the grace of God and His Son Jesus Christ that we can be saved* (Acts 4:12). We have to believe, to be saved. That takes faith.

Walking by faith and not by sight (2 Corinthians 5:7) makes all the difference when going through this life. When we walk by faith, we can have peace. I could go on and on about faith, but just think how it may affect people when they see your faith in God. Especially when you are going through hard times.

Next to the last of the fruits mentioned is **meekness**. Some definitions of meekness would be to be submissive, teachable, patient, and humble. I never considered myself as meek, but as The Holy Spirit has helped me to grow and learn, I can see these attributes growing in me and some that I already had.

Praise God! There are many scriptures which include meekness. Here is one of my favorites; In Galatians 6:1 KJV it says, *"Brethren, if a man be overtaken in a fault, ye which are spiritual, restore such a one in the spirit of meekness, considering thyself, lest thou also be tempted."*

The last fruit of the Spirit mentioned is ***temperance***. This one covers much more than I initially realized. Temperance defined is: (1) moderation in action, thought or feeling: restraint. (2a) habitual moderation in the indulgence of the appetites or passions. (2b) moderation in or abstinence from the use of alcoholic beverages (Merriam-Webster Dictionary).

Think about this one as a Christian whose testimony and witness are on the line, due to our behaviors in front of others, especially the unbelievers. People expect Christians to differ than worldly people. God expects us to be different too. Be sanctified (set apart) unto The Lord.

End of Chapter Thoughts: All of these fruits which come from The Holy Spirit are to be evident in a Christian's life as we grow from glory to glory. How can you be sure they are growing in you?

CHAPTER EIGHT
Hearing From God

First, I want to share some testimonials of my own on hearing from God through dreams, visions, and other ways that He communicates with me. The first memory I have of receiving a dream from God was in the 1980s. I had been feeling led to do some fasting, but had not followed through.

One night I had a dream of Jesus and I standing about 20 feet apart from each other, in a large empty space. He was pointing His finger at me and repeatedly and slowly saying to me, "*Fast, fast, fast.*" That inspired and motivated me so much that the very next day I was able to fast without much trouble. I have been able to grow in my fasting since then.

Over time, I began to hear clearly from The Lord and eventually began to have visions. The Lord would speak to me as I was driving down the road, usually in response to a question I asked Him. Sometimes, He would speak directly to me, through others, or through His Word.

When I was in my early twenties, I had a visit from some people that had caused me some confusion concerning parts of the bible. I asked God to help me because I didn't want to be confused. I hadn't been up to that point. I was raised in church my entire life and had been taught the truth of the Gospel.

I heard of individuals opening their bible and getting an obvious word from The Lord, but had never experienced it for myself. I opened the bible and God spoke loud and clear to me from 2 Timothy, telling me to continue, that from a child, I had known the scriptures that are able to make me wise unto salvation through faith which is in Christ Jesus (2 Timothy 3:15). The confusion left. I now love sharing the Gospel with others, knowing that His truth will set them free.

One of my favorite testimonies of that is when I had been unfairly let go from a position, I knew God had placed me in. As I left there for the last time, heading to our little green church in Pacific Beach, California, The Praise Center, I said to God, "I'm just going to believe You are taking me forward."

We were in the middle of a revival. As I entered, I decided to sit in the back since the service had already begun. I had not spoken to anyone. After church, a prophet of The Lord approached me and told me that The Lord had a word for me. This is what God said to me, *"You go ahead, and you believe that I am taking you forward."*

Exactly what I said to Him alone in my car. He said some more encouraging words to me after that. I was blessed! I am blessed!

God often likes to speak to us in the middle of the night. It seems that 3:00 a.m. is a favorite of His. Many can testify of this. I've heard of it often. Sometimes He speaks to me when I am halfway between sleep and awake, more awake than asleep. But the visions I've had have all been while I was awake. Some were when I just woke up, and some when I was wide awake (I shared the one of hugging Jesus in a previous chapter).

One vision was of a map of the United States which had a large, capital letter C in the middle of it. I automatically knew that God was calling me to intercede for this country I live in. I didn't know why at the time, but I knew He had good reason to ask me (and others) to specifically pray and intercede for The United States of America. I can now see many reasons why.

One of my favorite visions was of my dad, right after his passing. It had only been minutes; I was on the phone with my younger sister, Ginger. We had just received news of our dad's passing and were on the phone, taking in the news and supporting each other. Ginger said, "Just think! Dad is probably dancing with mom right now."

Our mom had passed away years before. While growing up, we would be entertained with an occasional dance by our parents (the two step). They could really move! What a nice memory. But, just as Ginger said those words, God gave me a vision. I heard The Lord say, "*No.*" At that very moment I saw my dad bowed down at Jesus' feet.

Simultaneously, I heard The Lord say, "*This is what is important, and this is what he is doing.*"

INSIGHT

God then revealed to me what my dad was saying to Jesus. "Thank You for even allowing "me" to be here!"

My dad was wearing a tannish colored gown, gathered at the waist. His face was flat on the floor and his hands stretched out to Jesus' feet. My dad's hair was pitch black. Jesus was barefoot. He was sitting. I saw Him from His lap down. The area they were in was large and empty except for them. The floor was very shiny. I saw and heard all this in a split second! Of course, I told my sister.

There are also what is called "open visions." These happen when you are fully awake, and your eyes are wide open. You see things in the physical. For example, some have seen angels and even spoken to them. I have never seen or spoken to an angel, but I do have other experiences of open visions. I'll share one of my favorites.

One of my favorite scriptures in the bible is Psalm 46:10, *"Be still and know that I am God."* God had spoken this to me years ago while going through a tough time. I waited on The Lord for 10 years and received my miracle! Yes, it was worth the wait.

When I experienced this open vision, I was actually taking a friend's dog for a walk in the middle of the day. After receiving a text message that I wasn't sure how I should answer, I asked The Lord what I should do. I took about 3 steps and, on the sidewalk, right in front of me was a very large, shiny, red rectangle with bright yellow numbers in the middle of it. The numbers were 4610 (Psalm 46:10)! I couldn't miss this painting. I had just passed the same area minutes before and was on my way back to where our walk began when I saw it. How could I have missed it? I said, "Lord, is this you?" And so, I waited.

The issue with the text resolved itself. Two days later, I took that same walk and I said to The Lord, "That would be something if that isn't even there." I hadn't thought of it as possibly being a miraculous open vision from God until that very moment. I just thought it was a new painting of someone's address. As I rounded the corner and walked towards that same area, I saw that it was not there! There was no sign of it ever being there. I was so excited to know that God had answered my question in such an awesome way. Each time I took that walk after that, I just marveled as I passed that spot. What an awesome God I serve!

God wants to speak to each of us, and I believe He does. We just don't always recognize His voice. But we can. The bible says that His sheep hear His voice. It seems to almost always be when I am alone that I hear God speak to me. There are exceptions, of course. He can speak to us whenever He chooses.

Hearing from God is one of the highlights of my life. If you want to experience hearing His voice for yourself, tell Him. Then be sure to spend some quiet time in His presence. Communication is a two-way street. After talking to Him, sit quietly. Don't get in a hurry. Try not to get distracted with phone calls, etc. Make an appointment with God. I desire to do this more myself.

INSIGHT

My husband, Pastor Richard S. Hull Jr., always says that God has a great sense of humor. That is not the way we typically view God, but I believe it is a part of His personality. We are made in His image. We possess His attributes. Humor is one of those. He is definitely a mighty and awesome God! He is all powerful (omnipotent), everywhere at once (omnipresent) and an all-knowing God (omniscient). He is the ONLY one who can save.

He is The One who created the heavens and the earth. But He also is loving, compassionate, understanding, forgiving, and much more, including humorous. Here is an example some of you may have a hard time believing, but you can believe it.

I had awakened on a Sunday morning and wasn't feeling up to getting ready to go anywhere. I think I was just really tired. Well, I pushed myself to get ready and made it to church. As I was standing at my usual place, the front pew, I had my hands up worshipping God. It was during the praise and worship service, and I was feeling The Lord's presence so sweetly. I said to God, "I'm so happy that I made it to church today."

He said to me very clearly, *"Give me five!"*

I was surprised for a moment, but then said, "Okay Lord," and raised my hand toward heaven and gave Him "five." I then went on to testify of the experience during testimonial time. People got a good chuckle out of it, but because they knew and trusted me, I believe most believed it.

Now, before you judge me, let me ask a question and explain

a couple of things. Why limit God? Just because that is not a common thing we hear about God, it doesn't mean He can't speak to us any way He chooses. I have learned that He interacts with us according to our personalities, our understanding, and our ability to receive from Him. I obviously am pretty open-minded to allowing God to "be Himself" with me. I think He appreciates that. I also know the reason He said, "*Give me five!*" was because during that time period, it was something that I said to others often. I still do sometimes. Yes, God has a great sense of humor.

I often hear God speak to me as I am laying in my bed, just waking up. I have heard Him while driving in my car. I have heard Him just sitting in my living room. I believe when we are open-minded about God communicating with us one on one, He will do that. Open your mind to the fact that God can, and He does. Open your heart to receive a word from Him. Ask Him with a sincere heart.

End of Chapter Thoughts: Document any dreams or visions you have experienced. Write down times you felt or knew God was speaking to you. If you have not experienced any obvious communication back from Him, write what you would love to experience in this area.

INSIGHT

CHAPTER NINE
Troubles, Trials, And Temptations

Psalm 34:17 KJV says, *"The righteous cry, and the Lord heareth, and delivereth them out of all their troubles."* God never promised us a rose garden, as the saying goes. But He did say in His word that He would bring us out of all our troubles, and He will never leave us nor forsake us. He did say that we can have eternal life, living in His presence forever. God allows us to be tried, but it is the enemy that tests us.

The enemy's goal through our testing is to cause us to get distracted from our relationship with God and to fall away from Him. To prove us unfaithful to God. The enemy's goal is also to defeat us and destroy us. God's goal is to prove us faithful. He wants to make sure that we are going to serve Him no matter what comes our way. He wants to see us continuing to love Him and trust Him, no matter what.

Also, the trying of our faith strengthens us, and He knows that we need to be strong to make it to the end without giving up. We can't be fair weathered friends of God and expect to make it to the end. We have to be rooted in Christ. No matter the storms of life, I shall not be moved!

INSIGHT

In my experience, I have seen that there is a difference between a trial and a right-out spiritual attack from demonic forces. A trial is something that we pray ourselves "through." An attack of the enemy is something that we can pray ourselves "out" of. We need to go through our trials in faith, praising God and knowing that His grace is sufficient for us. He says that *in our weaknesses, His strength is made perfect* (2 Corinthians 12:9).

We need His strength to be poured out on us when we are weak. We are blessed to have His grace available to us. When going through a trial, be sure to ask The Lord to help you learn what it is that He is wanting to teach you through it. (I like to pray that I learn quickly!) If we pray ourselves "out" of a trial rather than "through" a trial, we may just have to repeat it later. And we will continue to be tested in that same area until we are victorious over it.

Once we are the victor, we grow and then can move forward in The Lord. But I always say, *if it wasn't this trial, it would be another*. I might as well deal with the one I'm in and still try to be content knowing that my faith is being tested, and I want to pass this test victoriously. Especially if it is one that actually has been going on for a while. I just think to myself, *well, at least I'm used to this one*.

The bible says to encourage yourself daily. That thinking helps to encourage me. It has also been used to encourage others that feel stuck in a trial. There are times when we are under a spiritual attack and we do not get immediate deliverance. In that instance, we will need to pray ourselves through, as well as out. We may need to add fasting to our prayers for deliverance. We may need to call in reinforcements. There is power in numbers.

We are to *submit to God, resist the enemy, and he will flee* (James 4:7 KJV). We can *put on the garment of praise for the spirit of heaviness* (Isaiah 61:3). I have been tested in various ways and have received some insight from The Holy Spirit on how to combat the enemy in those different scenarios. I'll share some examples.

When Being Tempted: The Bible says that God *will not allow us to be tempted above that we are able (to resist), but with every temptation, He will provide a way of escape* (1 Corinthians 10:13). What I have learned is that even though God provides a way out for us, we have to be willing to take that escape route.

The enemy, of course, does not play fair. Ever. He will also tempt us not to accept the way out that God has so graciously provided for us. The enemy double tempts us. He tempts us to sin and then he tempts us to give in and ignore God's convictions in us. The way out? Don't go near it, don't pass by it, don't even look at it! Go the other direction.

When Feeling Depression: *Put on the garment of praise for the spirit of heaviness* (Isaiah 61:3 KJV). Pray, praise, meditate on the goodness of God. Listen to praise and worship music. Read God's Word. Read God's Word out loud. Reach out to a trusted, Godly friend. Someone stronger than you in the faith is preferable. Then you will get good counsel. Get up out of that bed and help someone else who is in need. This takes strength. God's strength, but He says that *His strength is made perfect in our weakness. His grace is sufficient for us. When you have done all you can to stand, stand therefore* (Ephesians 6:3-14)

When Feeling Oppression: This is an outright attack of the enemy. He has no right over God's children. This means war! It's time to call in reinforcements again. It's time to get your Shield of Faith activated! It's time to remember who and Whose you are. God is our source, and we should never depend on anyone more than we depend on Him. But He does use us for each other. Remember, *greater is He that is in you than he that is in the world* (1 John 4:4). We can bind the enemy and loose God's deliverance over ourselves. Matthew 16:19 KJV says, *"And I will give unto thee the keys of the kingdom of heaven: and whatsoever thou shalt bind shall be bound in heaven: and whatsoever thou shalt loose on earth shall be loosed in heaven."* Proclaim your victory, in Jesus' Name!

When feeling other outright spiritual attacks (this means war again!) It should be obvious that it is a spiritual attack, but we don't always realize that at first. You may think you need to see a doctor at first, but give it a try. Stand on God's promises. Bind those demons in the mighty name of Jesus! Loose deliverance, peace, and the mind of Christ! Don't put it off. Deal with the enemy of your soul, ASAP. Even if you are feeling weak, begin. Start praying, resisting, and believing. Stand on God's word.

Remember, The Bible is our sword and one of our most

powerful weapons against the enemy. Our faith makes all our weaponry work. Take up that shield of faith! Don't believe the lies of the enemy. Know this attack is temporary. Bind and loose, bind and loose, in the mighty name of Jesus.

These attacks can materialize in various ways. Feeling irritable out of the blue to feeling suicidal. From anxiety to fear. These are emotions that are put on us unexpectedly. We can also have emotions that derive from the lies of the enemy. But remember who you are and Who you belong to. Proclaim that! Even out loud, "I am a child of The Most High God!" Say it in faith, believing it will make a difference and I believe that it will. I have experienced it firsthand.

I was under a tremendous spiritual attack. The spirit of oppression, I believe. It was very heavy, and I couldn't shake it. I spoke and prayed with a few Christian friends and family to no avail. I kept trying to push through. I wasn't going to just sit there and let the enemy continue affecting me and my day. But it was getting late, and I had already missed a day of work because the oppression was so heavy on me.

It was at the end of the day and I was watching a women's conference on television. The woman leading the conference wasn't even saved as far as I could tell (I had been listening to her for some years). She started encouraging the ladies in the audience to stand up and claim their position in life. Whether they were a stay-at-home mom or had a career outside of home. No matter their ethnic background, education, or income.

As I lay on the bed watching and listening to these women

standing up, one by one, stating their name and their position in life. I felt led to get up and do the same thing. I began walking back and forth in front of that television saying out loud, "My name is Carla, and I am a child of The Most High God! My name is Carla, and I am a child of The Most High God!" over and over as I was walking back and forth in front of that television. As I continued, I began feeling the presence of The Holy Spirit. I began to feel stronger. Before I knew it, that spirit of oppression left me! God honored my fight of faith that day.

That wasn't the only time I battled the spirit of oppression. I fought it spiritually and was victorious that time too. I went to a place by myself to pray, bind, and loose. I also went to church and had the elders there pray a prayer of deliverance over me. I was set free before I left the church. Praise God! I want to encourage you not to give up when in battle. Stay in faith, expecting.

We can battle any demonic attack because God has given us authority over demons and also instructions in His word on how to do that. Ephesians says that we wrestle not against flesh and blood but against spiritual wickedness. Our battles are with principalities. We have to fight them spiritually, using the name of Jesus. We can fight spiritually for others too. Interceding for them. Fasting for them. Believing for them. Encouraging them. Reminding them that this too shall pass.

One of my favorite scriptures is Isaiah 61:1 KJV, *"The Spirit of the Lord God is upon me; because the Lord has anointed me to preach good tidings unto the meek; He hath sent me to bind up the brokenhearted, to proclaim liberty to the captives, and the opening of the prison to them that are bound.*" One way to be victorious over your own trials and tribulations is to reach out to others and be a vessel of honor to God for them.

As God uses you to encourage and uplift others, He will also encourage and uplift you. The best thing we can do is to continue to go forward in God. The worse thing we could ever do, is to give up and walk away from God.

End of Chapter Thoughts: List your own trials, victories, and how God has used you to help others.

INSIGHT

CHAPTER TEN
Trusting God

There is a difference between having faith in God and trusting God, although it does take faith to trust. Faith is believing He will do what you ask of Him. That He will always be with you. That Jesus is The Son of God Who died and was resurrected so we can have eternal life, as we accept that gift from Him. Believing when we can't see it. Pressing through to believe when the enemy is bringing doubt. There are so many other things that we have faith for. Just believing without doubting.

Trust, on the other hand, is believing that whatever His plan is, it will be the perfect answer for the best outcome for you. In trusting God, we approve of His choices for our lives, because we know that He knows our future. We actually "trust His judgement." We submit to Him fully.

I was going through a very challenging time when The Lord spoke to me and asked me a question. He asked, *"What if I don't give you what you have been believing Me for? Will you trust that what I have for you is what is best for you?"*

That is the day I learned the difference between faith and trust. Until then, I always viewed them in the same category. I said, "Yes Lord," and went on with my day. I did not know what He had in store for me. What I was believing for at that time, and what God ultimately gave me, was quite a surprise. And I consider it a miracle to this day.

What He gave me was much more of a blessing to my life than what I had been believing Him for. It was like I was limiting what I could receive because I was believing for less than what was available to me. I didn't realize it at the time, but I am so thankful that God had a better plan for me.

Of course, there are other areas in our lives when we need to show God that we trust Him; when we get bad news, when we are stressing over things going on in our lives, a loved one dies, financial hardships, marital problems, or children out in sin. We do need to walk by faith during these times, but also trusting that He is always near to those who love and serve Him. *He will never leave us nor forsake us* (Hebrews 13:5 KJV). It definitely is a battle. Our flesh is fighting against our spirit. *The spirit indeed is willing, but the flesh is weak* (Matthew 26:41 KJV).

Are you waiting for a breakthrough in your life? Are you believing? Walking in faith? That is great! But remember, also trusting God, no matter the outcome, is the bigger challenge and a huge blessing. It brings with it peace of knowing God really does have good plans for us. We can believe He is always up to something good on our behalf. Even when we don't understand, we can place everything in His very capable hands.

***End of Chapter Thoughts*:** What does trusting God mean to you?

INSIGHT

CHAPTER ELEVEN
The Harvest/Winning Souls

I said to God, "I want to do something for you too." I was sitting in church and it was testimony time. One of the saints was sharing how The Lord was using them. All of a sudden, this desire hit me. "But what can I do?" I asked The Lord. I'm always at home. At that time, I was a housewife, mom, and childcare provider in my home.

During altar call, The Lord spoke to me through the pastor and said, *"I will send others to you who are down heartened and discouraged, and when they leave you, they will be uplifted and encouraged."*

That word from God came to fruition immediately, and I began my work for The Lord. It was the beginning of my ministry, which has grown over the past 30-plus years, to the point where the harvest is now the priority. I still have the gift of encouragement along with other gifts for ministry, which The Lord has anointed me for, but the Harvest is God's heart and now mine!

In Luke, chapter 10 verse 2 KJV it reads, *"The harvest truly is great but the labourers are few. Pray ye therefore, the Lord of the harvest, that He would send forth labourers into His harvest."*

Who is the harvest? The harvest is those who are ready to accept Jesus as their Lord and Savior, but need someone to guide them to salvation.

Who will guide them? The labourers of God.

Who are the labourers? God's people that go out to share the gospel of Jesus Christ to win souls. *The fruit of the righteous is a tree of life and he that winneth souls is wise* (Proverbs 11:30 KJV).

When The Holy Spirit really began to teach me how to go about winning souls, I had been trying to witness to others about getting saved, but I was not getting very far. One night He gave me a dream that opened my understanding to what I needed to do different. In my dream there was a large fish tank that was about a quarter of the way filled with water. In the water were quite a few large gray fish. They were flopping around, trying to survive in that small amount of water. The Lord then spoke to me. He said, *"You are giving them just enough to survive until you can get back to them."*

I knew He was talking about the souls I had been trying to witness to. This insight had such an impact on me and the way I began to share the gospel. I knew He was instructing me to give people (the harvest) all of the information they needed to be saved the first time I witnessed to them. I also realized that I had no guarantee that I would ever have a second opportunity to speak to those same individuals about The Lord again. And so, I began giving them the "whole kit and caboodle." That is everything they needed to know for salvation and the opportunity to receive Christ as their Savior, right then.

I was so surprised and blessed as people began saying yes, most without hesitation! Occasionally, someone would not be ready, that is when we plant a seed or water one that someone else already planted. Prayerfully, these will become part of the Harvest as well. We need to be willing to reach out to the harvest. God will bring the increase.

Be careful not to let the enemy convince you of any of his reasons not to tell someone about Jesus. Jesus said in Mark 16:15, *"Go ye into all the world and preach the gospel to every creature."*

How many times have you heard someone say, "Be careful, you don't want to offend them or scare them away?"

Well, I believe that is a trick of the devil to keep us from preaching the gospel to every creature. If the name of Jesus offends someone, then sobeit. We need to obey God's word. Everyone has the right and absolutely needs to hear the gospel of Jesus Christ, which is able to make them wise unto salvation. After they have heard, then they have free choice to receive or to reject Jesus, The Messiah, and eternal life. *Neither is there salvation in any other: for there is none other name under heaven given among men, whereby we must be saved* (Acts 4:12 KJV).

INSIGHT

Pray for God to send the right person to your lost family members. Our loved ones don't always receive from us. In Mark 6:4, it says that *a prophet is not (without) honor but in his own country.* That means away from home a prophet receives honor more than in his own home. In other people's lives we would be more respected and heard than from our own family. So, we reach out to others, to their loved ones, and pray they will reach out to ours.

Our example to our own family needs to be how we walk the walk rather than how we talk the talk. That is very important and will have the most impact. I had one of my daughters say to me, "Mom, you are the best Christian I have ever known!"

My reply was, "Wow! and you live with me and know my faults!" What an eye opener that was. What a blessing!

Remember, the harvest is God's heart. He wants us to reap while *"it is day."* We need to go out and win those souls while we still have time. Help the harvest get saved before it is too late! They want to go to heaven but need some direction. That is where we come in. We can and should be the labourers that God sends out.

He will open doors to give you opportunities to lead someone to Jesus. He will lead you to His harvest. The ones who are ready to say yes. Pray that God gives you a burden for the lost. Pray that He gives you boldness to speak up. Pray for divine appointments continually. He has done this with me. My heart aches for the lost. Let's go rescue some souls together. In Jesus' name, amen!

End of Chapter Thoughts: What are some ways you can prepare to go out into the harvest and labour to win souls? Remembering that "*He who wins souls is wise* (Proverbs 11:30)."

INSIGHT

CHAPTER TWELVE
Sin/Separation From God & Unforgiveness

"*Behold, the Lord's hand is not shortened, that it cannot save; neither His ear heavy, that it cannot hear: But your iniquities have separated between you and your God, and your sins have hid His face from you, that he will not hear* (Isaiah 59:1,2 KJV)."

In John 9:31 KJV it says, "*Now, we know that God heareth not sinners: but if any man be a worshipper of God, and doeth His will, him he heareth.*"

We have to go through Jesus to be heard by God. *It is the blood of Jesus that cleanses us from all sin and unrighteousness* (1 John 1:7, 9 KJV). Once we have accepted the sacrifice Jesus did on the cross, asking Him to forgive us of all our sins and accepting Him as our Savior, then the communication is open between us and God. When Jesus took our punishment and died as the ultimate sacrifice for our sins, He reconciled us to God. *Now, we can go boldly to God's throne* (Hebrews 4:16).

Once we have asked Jesus to forgive us of our sins, then we

too need to forgive those who have hurt or offended us or our loved ones in any way. The Lord's prayer says, *"Forgive us our debts (trespasses) 'as' we forgive our debtors (those who have trespassed against us)*. In Matthew 6:15 it says to forgive others so that God will forgive us (paraphrased). It says, if we do not forgive others, neither will God forgive us. This is mandatory. Not a suggestion, not optional if you want to be forgiven by God.

Forgiveness is a choice. It does not depend on how you "feel." To forgive means you stop holding a grudge. It means the other person owes you nothing. Not even an apology. Although apologies are nice, it is not necessary when choosing to forgive. Even if the person has already passed, you can choose to forgive. This is between you and God. It does not necessarily mean all the negative feelings have left that memory. It just means letting go of your bitterness toward that person. Hate the wrong that was done, but not the person.

The last thing we want to do is "allow" anything or anyone to come between us and God. It's just not worth it. We have free choice. God says *He will never leave or forsake us*, but if sin and unforgiveness separates us from Him, *then we need to repent (turn away) from those things*. It is up to us. He is there just waiting for us to make the right choices. Concentrate on bettering your relationship with The Lord. It is a beautiful thing to draw nearer to God.

If you are having difficulty forgiving someone, start by asking God to forgive you for that. Ask Him to help you because you want to be forgiven by Him. Tell Him you choose to forgive but are having a hard time with it. He will help you if you are sincere. The Lord taught me, it's just a choice. So, I choose to forgive everyone who has hurt me or my loved ones. I refuse to hold a grudge. I pray they all make it to heaven. Yes, even the really bad ones can be saved. Just like any one of us. They only have to be sincere, ask Jesus to forgive them, repent, turn away from sin, and do their best to obey God's word.

Once you come out of sin and into open communication with God, The Father, you can talk to Him about whatever is on your heart and mind, and He will hear you. He says in His word, *"If My people, which are called by My name, shall humble themselves, and pray, and seek My face, and turn from their wicked ways; then will I hear from heaven, and will forgive their sin and will heal their land,"* (2 Chronicles 7:14 KJV).

Notice He says "**then**" will I hear from heaven, and will forgive their sin, and will heal their land. There are prerequisites to being forgiven by God. *Not everyone who says, "Lord, Lord," will make it to heaven* (Matthew 7:21). We must come out of sin, forgive others, and accept Jesus as our Savior, the ONLY way to heaven.

Jesus is our advocate (1 John 2:1 KJV), and yes, we are living under mercy and grace, but we are not to trample on that grace just because we have Jesus' blood to cleanse us. If we call ourselves Christians but continue in sin, what makes us any different than the heathen (sinners)? We are to come out and be a separate people. A peculiar people for our God because we don't fit in with the worldly ways anymore. We rise above it because since *we have been born again, the old has passed away, behold all things are new* (2 Corinthians 5:17). Even sinners expect us to be different. If we are not, what do they perceive? What kind of example do we become to them? Hypocritical, I would answer.

If we really want a close and personal relationship with our Lord, we MUST come out, and stay out, of a sinful life. Don't waste the years God has allotted you. Work as unto The Lord. Ask Him, "What can I do for You today, Lord?" Because only what we do for Christ will last. Everything else is temporary.

End of Chapter Thoughts: After reading this chapter, has The Holy Spirit revealed areas that you need to ask for forgiveness, or people you need to forgive?

CHAPTER THIRTEEN
Live Ready

We need to be living ready for Christ's return. *In the twinkling of an eye, when we think not, and like a thief in the night, the trumpet will sound and the dead in Christ will rise first.*

1 Thessalonians 4:16 KJV says, "*For the Lord Himself shall descend from heaven with a shout, with the voice of the archangel, and with the trump of God: and the dead in Christ shall rise first.*" Then verse 17 goes on to say, "*Then we which are alive and remain shall be caught up together with them in the clouds, to meet the Lord in the air: and so shall we ever be with the Lord.*"

Will you be ready? Are you ready? Do you KNOW that you are going to heaven? How can you be sure?

The bible says in Romans 10:9,10 KJV, "*⁹ If you confess with your mouth the Lord Jesus and believe in your heart that God has raised Him from the dead you will be saved. ¹⁰ For with the heart one believes unto righteousness and with the mouth confession is made unto salvation.*"

Also, in John 3:16-17 it says, "*¹⁶ For God so loved the world that He gave His only begotten Son, that whosoever believes in*

Him should not perish but have everlasting life [17] *for God did not send His Son into the world to condemn the world, but that the world through Him might be saved."*

A simple prayer to salvation: Dear Jesus, I believe that You are the Son of God and that you died for my sins and were raised from the dead by Your Heavenly Father. I ask for forgiveness now for all my sins. I ask that You come into my heart and be my Lord and Savior. I accept You now. In Jesus' Name, Amen.

If you said this prayer from your heart, you are now born again. Saved! A child of God! Heaven bound! Your name is now written in The Lambs Book of Life. The angels of heaven are dancing around God's throne in celebration of you! Praise God! Find a good bible teaching church to help you grow in your new relationship with God, The Father, The Son, and The Holy Spirit.

Read the Bible. It is one way that God speaks to us. Listen to good Christian music. It will help feed your soul. You now need some spiritual food to be able to grow into a mature Christian. This takes time, but don't give up. Just do your best and ask for forgiveness when you need to. It will be worth it in the end.

If you are still not quite sure, or just want a little more understanding, please see the last chapter of this book, "The Salvation Chapter." Jesus is coming back for His children. The Church. Don't be left behind. Now you can begin the process of living ready. Ready for the return of the Messiah, our Lord and Savior, Jesus Christ. I hope whoever reads this book reads it in time.

Now, to the more mature Christian. Those of us who have already been saved and serving The Lord. There are so many scriptures (most of them) written to us that will teach us to live a life pleasing to The Lord. There are scriptures that let us know how "we" can be sure to make it to heaven, too. The Word says *they that endure to the end shall be saved* (Matthew 10:22), t*here is no more sacrifice for a willful sin* (Hebrews 10:26), and t*o forgive others or God will not forgive you* (Matthew 6:15).

Once we have been saved and forgiven of "all" our sins, we then have a responsibility to live as holy of a life, unto God, as we can. When we give in to any temptation, (being tempted is not a sin, giving in to it is) ask forgiveness and walk away from it (repent). We cannot expect to confess, be saved, and then purposely choose to live in sin. A willful sin. After we have come to the knowledge that something is sin, it is a sin to us. We cannot "have our cake and eat it too." Don't fall to this lie from the enemy.

Live ready means to be watching for Jesus' return. As if it will be any moment. Don't have your back turned to the window, distracted with this world. *Be watchful, lest you be caught unaware* (Luke 21:34). What do you want to be doing when that trumpet sounds? What do you "not" want to be doing when Jesus returns? This is where the tires meet the road. The bottom line. Are you, oh Christian, certain you are ready to meet your Savior? Whether it be during the rapture or through a physical death, we will. The Bible says that *tomorrow is not promised. This life is as a vapor* (James 4:14 KJV), here today but gone tomorrow.

Jesus spoke in parables many times to help the people understand. In Matthew 13:11 KJV, when the disciples asked why, Jesus replied, *"Because it is given unto you to know the mysteries of the kingdom of heaven, but to them it is not given."* What He was telling them was that through The Holy Spirit, they had been given insight to the secrets of the kingdom of God, but to others it had not been revealed.

One example of Jesus' teaching through a parable is in this passage from Matthew 13:3-8 KJV, *"³ And He spake many things to them in parables saying, behold a sower went forth to sow; ⁴ and when he sowed, some seeds fell by the way side, and the fowls came and devoured them up: ⁵ some fell upon stony places, where they had not much earth: and forthwith they sprung up, because they had no deepness of earth: ⁶ and when the sun was up, they were scorched; and because they had no root they withered away. ⁷ And some fell among thorns; and the thorns sprung up and choked them: ⁸ but other fell into good ground, and brought forth fruit.*

In that parable, the seed represents God's word, and the soil represents us (our hearts). In the same chapter beginning with verse 19 He explains that parable further, *"¹⁹ When anyone heareth the word of the kingdom, and understandeth it not, then cometh the wicked one and catcheth away that which was sown in his heart. This is he which received seed by the wayside. ²⁰But he that received the seed into stony places, the* *same is he that heareth the word, and anon with joy receiveth it; ^{21} yet hath he not root in himself, but dureth for a while; for when tribulation or persecution ariseth because of the word, by and by he is offended. ^{22}He also that received seed among the thorns is he that heareth the word; and the care of this world, and the deceitfulness of riches, choke the word, and he becometh unfruitful. ^{23}But he that received seed into the good ground is he that heareth the word, and understandeth it; which also beareth fruit and bringeth forth, some a hundredfold, some sixty, some thirty.* (See chapter 7 on the fruit of the Spirit)

This is our divine opportunity to live ready for the return of the Messiah, The Lord Jesus Christ. He will come to take His children with Him. Those left behind will have a tremendously hard time. Even those who know better may be too emotionally caught up in what is happening during that time to make right choices. If you are left behind, DO NOT take the Mark of the Beast! You will be lost forever if you do. No matter how hard it gets. It will be almost impossible, but those who can stand strong and resist will make it.

That is why I want to stress, live ready! It is so much easier now than it will be then. No matter what is going on in your life right now, now is the time. Today is the day of salvation. Be sure to be watching for *Jesus' appearing in the clouds* (Mark 13:26, 14:62). Live ready so you can know this next scripture applies to you; 1 Thessalonians 4:17 KJV, "*Then we, which are alive and remain, shall be caught up together with them in the clouds, to meet the Lord in the air: and so shall we ever be with the Lord.*" Hallelujah!

INSIGHT

End of Chapter Thoughts: What kind of soil are you? Are you living ready?

CHAPTER FOURTEEN
It's Time to Grow

The meat of The Word defines the deeper things of God and comes through revelation knowledge (insight), hearing The Word of God, trials and tribulations, among other things mentioned in this book. These things help to bring more understanding. These things can bring us closer to God if we allow them to. If we desire them to.

Through our experiences in walking with God, we learn to hear His voice. We learn to depend on Him. We learn to trust our God. Our experiences as a follower of Christ teach us how to overcome. Jesus is our example. He is The Word. He is our Savior. He is The Son of God and the ONLY way to The Father and eternal life. Hear this and know this! There is none other!

We do not need sugar coated sermons. We do not need to be careful with the truth. The truth will set us free. Jesus is the Truth. I believe God is saying, "*Grow up!*" Turn back to the window, away from the distractions of this life, and be watchful. Watch for the return of The Messiah. Our soon coming King. Don't be caught off guard. He asks in The Word if *He will find any faith on the earth when He returns* (Luke 18:8).

INSIGHT

If you truly want to grow, be open to The Holy Spirit and His guidance. Listen and obey. Follow His instructions. Ask The Lord to teach you what He wants you to learn and when He wants you to learn it. There is always more room for growth. I'm looking forward to more insight in my own life.

I want to share some other thoughts on things we should be doing to aid in our spiritual growth and maturity. If we really want to grow and to continue to grow, we should be sure to keep a close relationship with God. Remember, sin separates us from God, so we need to avoid allowing sin in our lives. Always ask for forgiveness and repent (turn away from sin).

Praying to God on a regular basis, daily, and multiple times during the day keeps communication going. Be sure to spend time listening for His voice, too. As you grow, you should be able to recognize His voice more easily and quicker too. He says in His word, *"My sheep hear My voice, and I know them, and they follow Me* (John 10:27 KJV)."

God uses trials to develop us. The enemy tries to use them to defeat us. As we are growing through trials and testing, troubles and tribulations, we are to guard our minds and hearts. We have our armour of God and we are to especially use our Shield of Faith. Using our faith brings peace. Having the peace of God protects our minds and hearts.

Be sure to keep a soft heart towards God so He can easily mold it. Trusting Him no matter what, even when we don't understand what is going on, will cause great growth. Be available to do His will through obedience to His word and to

The Holy Spirit. Be brave and courageous. Be determined. Be committed.

Stand in adversity by your faith. Endure temptation and you will be blessed. James 1:12 KJV says, *"Blessed is the man that endureth temptation, for when he is tried, he shall receive the crown of life, which the Lord hath promised to them that love Him."*

We all have areas that we are weaker in and will have to be tested so we can be proven faithful to God. But, *we are more than conquerors through Christ who strengthens us* (Romans 8:37 KJV), and then, growth! God wants us to grow in Him and so He will help us as we seek that growth and are obedient to Him.

We need to get rid of any pride, for pride comes before a fall—the opposite of growth. Be humble to receive wisdom, and wisdom will bring growth. Proverbs 11:2 KJV says, *"When pride comes, disgrace follows, but with humility comes wisdom."*

Reading the bible on a daily basis will teach you a lot too. As The Holy Spirit gives understanding, you will surely grow. Be obedient to His word. Be a faithful child of God. Be sure to give Him all your praise and worship, because He is more than worthy!

I remember when I first really noticed the prayer of Jabez in 1 Chronicles. I was able to apply it to my own life, and it was very useful in my faithfulness of praying, seeking more spiritual maturity, and being able to do more for The Lord. Below is that prayer, and then my prayer follows:

The Prayer of Jabez: 1 Chronicles 4:10, *And Jabez called on the God of Israel saying oh, that You would bless me indeed, and enlarge my territory, that Your hand would be with me, and that You would keep me from evil, that I may not cause pain!*

So, God granted him what he requested.

My Prayer: Lord, enlarge my boundaries so I can receive more from You, so that I can do more for You. Help me not to cause any pain. In Jesus' mighty name, Amen!

God answered Jabez' prayer, and he answered my prayer too. Because He did, I have been blessed to grow from glory to glory and now to bring this book to you for encouragement and some insight to help you in your own growth. Be blessed in Jesus' Mighty name, Amen!

End of Chapter Thought: So, if we want to grow spiritually, what are some ways to accomplish that? What should we do?

CHAPTER FIFTEEN
The Salvation Chapter

Again, we choose our eternal destiny, by either choosing Christ and entering into eternal life with God or to reject God's Son and spend eternity in the Lake of Fire, where God's presence will be absent forever. It's a choice. Your choice! If God is calling you, be alert! Be ready to answer that call while you can. Many are called but few are chosen. The day is coming when that option will be over, and sooner than later.

As an illustration, I'd like you to imagine death row. There are cells filled with people waiting to receive the punishment they deserve, death. They are all just waiting for their name to be called. All of a sudden, this "most wanted" criminal (who has been falsely accused) volunteers to give himself up on one condition. He asks that all of the other death row inmates have the opportunity to walk away free as he takes their place.

The warden says "deal" and orders this man to be scheduled for death as soon as possible. The warden then authorizes that all the cells be opened.

The inmates are told the condition of their release and many shout, "Hallelujah!" They then walk away free. No hesitation.

Others have a hard time believing it is true. They think there must be some kind of catch, so they stay in their cell, afraid to check it out. There are some who believe, but think they don't deserve to be set free and will not accept the offer. Still, there are others who are just plain rebellious. They don't need anyone doing them any favors! In the meantime, the ones who dared to believe, just enough to step out on faith and out of their cells, are now running free, never to be held accountable for their crimes again.

The only problem is this is a limited time offer. The freed inmates even come back to testify to the others that the freedom they have is real! This time, a few more step out of their cells on faith, and find out for themselves that it is true after all, and they rejoice. But there are still others, reluctant and unbelieving.

In the meantime, the clock is ticking. It is 5 till midnight. The call is about to go out to all who have accepted the free gift of this salvation. At midnight, the cells will once again close.

It is the same with us and the sacrifice Jesus made by taking our punishment for being sinful beings. It is a free gift, but there is a time limit on this offer. Please don't wait too long. It is simply an act of faith, and it is your choice. We are His creation, and when we yield our lives to Him and accept Him as our Lord and Savior, it is then that we become the children of God!

I love being the daughter of The Most High God! He is my Heavenly Father. He is my Provider. He is my Strength. He is

THE SALVATION CHAPTER

my Master. He is my Shelter. He is everything to me. He can be all of this to you too, as you yield your life to Him. Just ask Him to forgive you through Jesus' sacrifice on the cross. He can become your everything too.

John 3:16 says, *"For God so loved the world that He gave His only begotten Son that whosoever believeth in Him would not perish but have everlasting life."* Jesus is the only way to heaven (John 14:6), *"No one comes to The Father but by Me."*

So, if you are not saved (born again) and want to be, please say this prayer, sincerely from your heart, and you will be saved:

> Dear Jesus, I believe that You are The Son of God and that You died for my sins. I believe that you rose again and are seated at the right hand of God, The Father. I accept Your offer to cleanse me from my sins with Your blood. Please forgive me and come into my heart and my life. I receive You now, as my Lord and Savior. In Jesus' name! Amen.

If you prayed that prayer from your heart and sincerely meant it, you are now saved from eternal damnation and have become a child of God. You have received eternal life with Jesus. You are an heir with Christ. Communication with The Father is now wide open to you.

Now that your sins have been cast away into the Sea of Forgetfulness, He will never remember them against you. You are now a brand-new creature in Christ. *Old things have passed*

INSIGHT

away, behold all things are new (2 Corinthians 5:17).

   There is so much power in the name of Jesus. Don't limit or doubt that. Now, boldly go and confess to someone you trust, that Jesus is your Lord and Savior. Also, find a good bible believing church to join and help grow your new relationship with God. Today is the day of your salvation! Praise God!

End of Chapter Thought: Write the date here if you accepted Jesus for the first time or rededicated your life to Him.

Today Is My Day of Salvation!

_____/_____/_____

APPENDIX

This book shares a lot of the insight God has given me through the years, but there is so much more. If The Lord wills, I would love to share more. For now, this is what has been brought back to my memory. This is how I choose to live my life. As pleasing to The Lord as is possible within me.

Revelation knowledge that comes from The Holy Spirit gives us more understanding and wisdom in walking this walk we call Christianity. It teaches us more about the things of God. His will. His truths. His ways. It builds our faith. It helps us to have the knowledge we need to defeat the enemy of our souls.

We learn how to better reach out to others, loving them as ourselves. We come to realize how God truly sees and feels about this world and our role in it. We are in the world, but we are not of it. We are called to occupy until He comes back to rapture the church. God will give us insight into how to accomplish these things and more.

With what God teaches us, we can begin to mature spiritually and better be used of Him. Have you heard the quote, "God does not call the equipped, but he equips the called?" Through our experiences and the revelation knowledge He gives, we can become the equipped.

INSIGHT

What a blessing that is. I pray that you can read, understand, and apply the insights in this book to the maturing of your own relationship with The Lord. I pray that you will grow to the point of helping others with their growing pains. But remember, you can give them the tree, but you can't decorate it for them.

This is some of what God has taught me and now has called me to share these things with you. This book is your tree. I give it to you. Now it is up to you on how you apply it to your life. Or in other words, how will you decorate your tree? It is your choice.

GOSPEL HANDOUT

Do you KNOW that you are going to heaven? How can you be sure?

In the bible it says in **Romans 10:9-10**: ⁹If you confess with your mouth The Lord Jesus and believe in your heart that God has raised Him from the dead, you will be saved. ¹⁰For with the heart, one believes unto righteousness and with the mouth confession is made unto salvation.

John 3:16-17: ¹⁶For God so loved the world that He gave His only begotten Son, that whosoever believes in Him should not perish but have everlasting life. ¹⁷For God did not send His Son into the world to condemn the world, but that the world through Him might be saved.

A Simple Prayer to Salvation: Dear Jesus, I believe that You are The Son of God and that you died for my sins and were raised from the dead by Your Heavenly Father. I ask for forgiveness now for all my sins. I ask that You come into my heart and be my Lord and Savior. I accept You now. In Jesus' Name, Amen.

**If you said this prayer from your heart,
you're now born again. Saved! Praise God.**

Find a good bible teaching church to help you grow in your new relationship with God—The Father, Son, and Holy Spirit—The Trinity.

www.ingramcontent.com/pod-product-compliance
Lightning Source LLC
Chambersburg PA
CBHW060807050426
42449CB00008B/1582